Swimming Scientifically Taught

MAXWELL PRESS

Swimming Scientifically Taught

FRANK EUGEN DALTON

Instructor in Scientific Swimming at the Dalton Swimming School,
and Originator of the Dalton Method

MAXWELL PRESS

Chennai Trichy New Delhi

MAXWELL PRESS

This edition has been published in india by arrangement with Carson Books, UK

ISBN 978-93-90877-09-6 Maxwell Press

Printed and bound in India

No. 44, Nallathambi Street,
Triplicane, Chennai 600 005

MJP 1005

Publisher : C. Janarthanan

Publisher's Note

The legacy of a country is in its varied cultural heritage, historical literature, developments in the field of economy and science. The top nations in the world are competing in the field of science, economy and literature. This vast legacy has to be conserved and documented so that it can be bestowed to the future generation. The knowledge of this legacy is slowly getting perished in the present generation due to lack of documentation.

Keeping this in mind, the concern with retrospective acquiring of rare books has been accented recently by the burgeoning reprint industry. Maxwell Press is gratified to retrieve the rare collections with a view to bring back those books that were landmarks in their time.

In this effort, a series of rare books would be republished under the banner, "Maxwell Press". The books in the reprint series have been carefully selected for their contemporary usefulness as well as their historical importance within the intellectual. We reconstruct the book with slight enhancements made for better presentation, without affecting the contents of the original edition.

Most of the works selected for republishing covers a huge range of subjects, from history to anthropology. We believe this reprint edition will be a service to the numerous researchers and practitioners active in this fascinating field. We allow readers to experience the wonder of peering into a scholarly work of the highest order and seminal significance.

MAXWELL PRESS

FRANK EUGEN DALTON

TO MY FATHER

THE LATE CAPT. DAVIS DALTON

who swam the English Channel from Cape Grisnez near Boulogne, France, to Folkestone, England, August 16-17, 1890; whose enthusiasm and unflagging interest in all matters pertaining to swimming and life-saving have been excelled by none, and who was a faithful practitioner of the methods herein set forth, this book is affectionately dedicated by his son,

THE AUTHOR

CONTENTS

Part I—Introduction

Part II—Various Kinds of Strokes

Part III—Floating, Diving and Scientific Swimming

CONTENTS

ILLUSTRATIONS

ILLUSTRATIONS

ILLUSTRATIONS

PART I

INTRODUCTION

INTRODUCTION

THE IMPORTANCE OF SWIMMING

THAT all persons ought to know how to safeguard themselves when in deep water is becoming more and more recognized as time passes. While swimming is probably the oldest pastime known to man, and has had, and still has, its votaries in every country, civilized or uncivilized, it is curious that this most useful science should have been so much neglected.

For an adult person to be unable to swim points to something like criminal negligence; every man, woman and child should learn. A person who can not swim may not only become a danger to himself, but to some one, and perhaps to several, of his fellow beings. Children as early as the age of four may acquire the art; none are too young, none too old. Doctors recommend swimming as the best all-around exercise. It is especially beneficial to nervous people. Swimming reduces corpnleney, improves the figure, expands the lungs, improves the circulation of the blood, builds up general health, increases vitality, gives self-confidence in case of danger, and exercises all the muscles in the body at one time. As an aid to development of the muscular system, it excels other sports. Every muscle is brought into play.

In other important ways it is a useful, and even a necessary accomplishment; no one knows when he may be called upon for a prac tical test of its merits. The *Slocum* steamboat catastrophe in the East River, New York, several years ago, gave a melancholy example of what better knowledge of swimming might have done to save the lives of passengers. That awful tragedy, which plunged an entire city into mourning, was too appalling to have its details revived here, but, regardless of the fact that the life-preservers on board were found unfit for use, the loss of life would have been made much smaller had the unfortunate passengers known how to keep their heads above water until help arrived. Millions of people are transported yearly by river craft, and just for lack of knowledge of how to swim a repetition of the *Slocum* disaster might occur any summer.

Only about 20 per cent. of the entire population of the United States know how to swim. A visit to any of the beaches along the Atlantic coast will convince any one of this fact. There is no excuse for this ignorance, especially in a city like New York, with miles of water front and fine beaches at its very door; nor is there excuse in other places where an ocean, lakes and rivers afford opportunities for swimming.

Swimming is a tonic alike for muscle and brain. The smallest child and the weakest woman can enjoy it equally with the strongest man. When slaves of the desk and counting-house are looking forward for an all too brief vacation and seek the mountains or seashore to store up energy for another year's work, they should know how to swim. Poor, indeed, is the region which can not boast of a piece of water in which to take an invigorating plunge.

The importance of being able to swim was very generally recognized in ancient times, notably by the Romans. Roman youth, as early as the Republican era, when trained to bear arms, were made to include in their exercises bathing and swimming in the Tiber, where competitions were frequent. Cassius in his youth became renowned as a swimmer. Shakespeare, in a familiar passage, describes a race between him and Julius Cæsar, Cassius being made the speaker:

"I was born free as Cæsar; so were you:
We both have fed as well, and we can both
Endure the winter's cold as well as he.
For once, upon a raw and gusty day,
The troubled Tiber chafing with her shores,
Cæsar said to me, 'Dar'st thou, Cassius, now,
Leap in with me into this angry flood
And swim to yonder point?' Upon the word,
Accoutred as I was, I plunged in,
And bade him follow; so, indeed he did.
The torrent roared; and we did buffet it
With lusty sinews; throwing it aside
And stemming it with hearts of controversy;
But ere we could arrive the point propos'd,
Cæsar cried, 'Help me, Cassius, or I sink.'
I, as Æneas, our great ancestor,
Did from the flames of Troy upon his shoulder
The old Anchises bear, so, from the waves of Tiber
Did I the tired Cæsar: And this man
Is now become a god."

THE IMPORTANCE OF SWIMMING

Macaulay, in one of his "Lays of Ancient Rome," describes the scene which followed after Horatius had been left alone to face the troops of Lars Porsena, his codefenders having escaped across the bridge:

> "Never, I ween, did swimmer,
> In such an evil case,
> Struggle through such a raging flood
> Safe to the landing place,
> But his limbs were borne up bravely,
> By the brave heart within,
> And our good father Tiber
> Bore bravely up his chin."

It was not until the nineteenth century that swimming really became a science. In fact, it was only within the last half-century that a real awakening to its importance occurred. At the present day swimming has come to be regarded as an indispensable adjunct to the education of the young. In many parts of Europe it forms part of the school curriculum. Of such paramount importance is it there held to be that, on entering the army, the first thing taught a young recruit is swimming. On this side of the Atlantic its importance is becoming more evident daily.

That the benefits to be derived from it have manifested themselves to municipalities is evidenced by the fact that, in addition to free swimming baths on the water front of New York in summer, there have been established several indoor bathing pavilions which are open and accessible all the year round.

Swimming, aside from its importance as a possible means to self-preservation in case of shipwreck, the upsetting of pleasure-boats, or any of the numerous accidents that so frequently happen on the water, and also, on occasion, as a means of saving life, is not only one of the best physical exercises known, but when one swims for exercise he is also conscious of receiving great pleasure. Most other forms of exercise, after they have been participated in for some time, are apt to become something like efforts, or even hardships. Swimming, on the other hand, continues to be exhilarating.

Unfortunately, those who have been best able to teach the science of swimming, because of having technical knowledge and proficiency, have not made systematic attempts to disseminate knowledge through scientific methods.

In this respect the author claims to differ with most other instructors. He has endeavored, in this work, to treat the subject scientifically and to use simple and concise language. His success as a teacher is attested by thousands of pupils who have acquired the principles of a system long known as the Dalton system.

LEARNING BY THE BOOK

The question is often asked whether it is possible for a person to learn to swim by studying a book or a series of articles. Much depends on the person. In the case of a very nervous person, it is improbable that this may be satisfactorily accomplished, for it is then absolutely necessary that a pupil must have an instructor, in order, at the start, to obviate dread of the water.

Where this dread of water or nervousness does not exist in any marked degree, study of a work such as this may be of unlimited advantage. By carefully following its instructions it will be possible to become a very fair swimmer without the aid of an instructor or any second person.

Naturally, it is not claimed that a majority of such self-taught swimmers will ever become experts at the art, altho even this is possible in a great many cases; but there is a moral certainty that, with the exception of the aforementioned nervous beginners, a fair knowledge of the science of swimming may be attained in this manner. Numbers of very good swimmers have had no other tuition than which came from study of a book. Especially is this true when following the directions outlined in this book in the matter, first, of practising keeping the eyes and mouth open under water, which will eliminate all nervousness; and, second, in practising the movements used in the breast and back strokes, which are of inestimable aid when actually taking to the water.

Of course, where the swimmer desires to attain true scientific knowledge of the art, the beginner needs the aid of an instructor who may watch for and correct any faults noticeable, for the simple reason that bad habits once contracted are more difficult to eliminate later on.

If the lessons herein set forth are carefully followed, there is no reason why, with the exceptions before mentioned, one should not become a good swimmer.

PART II

VARIOUS KINDS OF STROKES

VARIOUS KINDS OF STROKES

THE BACK STROKE

It may seem odd to the beginner (and to a great many proficient swimmers, for that matter) that in teaching swimming by the Dalton system, I always begin by having pupils swim first on the back. Most instructors do just the reverse; but during fourteen years of a successful career in teaching, the proficiency of the discharged pupil has justified the method. There are a number of very good reasons why learners should begin by first swimming on the back. More especially is this true of nervous or timid pupils.

In the first place, the body floats more naturally and much easier on the back. In the breast stroke, which is the first one taught by most instructors, the head has to be kept out of the water and must be supported as dead weight by the rest of the body, as explained later on. On the contrary, in the back stroke, or swimming on the back, the head rests on the water and needs no support from any other member of the body.

For the same reason the face, being up and away from the water, the beginner encounters no difficulty in breathing, and there is no danger of the water entering the mouth, which is often the cause of much annoyance to new pupils.

Then, again, while on the back, as the face is turned upward, the beginner, especially in the case of a nervous person, gains confidence from the very fact that he is not constantly looking into the water. And also, in contradistinction to all other strokes in swimming, the arms and legs move together—both arms and legs performing practically the same movements at the same time.

Thus the pupil, realizing the comparative easiness and the absence of any difficulty in having mastered this stroke, is imbued with such confidence that it becomes simply a matter of time and practise to acquire all other forms of swimming that he may wish to learn.

The first thing I do with a beginner, after he or she has donned a bathing suit (a suit in one piece is preferable, as it will not interfere with breathing) is to get the pupil to lie on the back, at full length on the marble, with the heels together, the toes out, the hands at the side of the body. Placing myself back of the pupil's head, the hands are drawn, with the fingers bent, up along the body till they touch

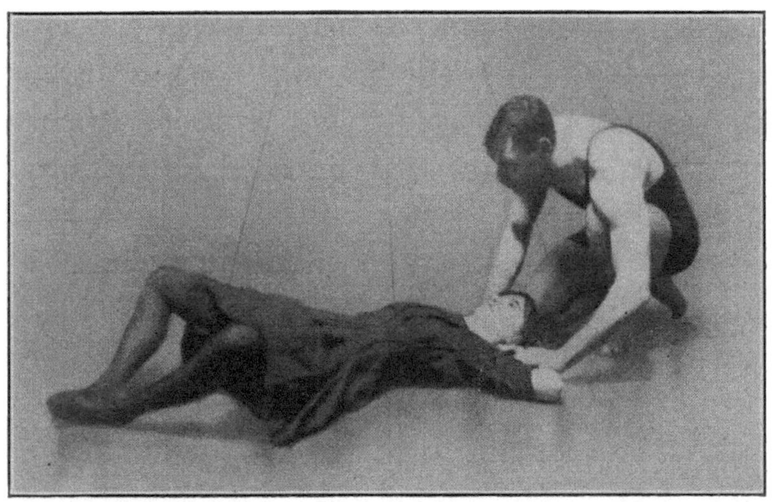

FIGURE 1

the shoulders (Fig. 1), the elbows being well turned out. Then the arms are straightened out horizontally from the shoulder, the palms of the hand down (Fig. 2). Then the arms, being rigid, are brought down sharply to the side of the body (Fig. 3). These movements should be repeated several times until the pupil gets accustomed to them.

Next the leg movements are shown. The heels are drawn up toward the body as far as possible with the knees well turned out (Fig. 4); the pupil then kicks the legs apart as far

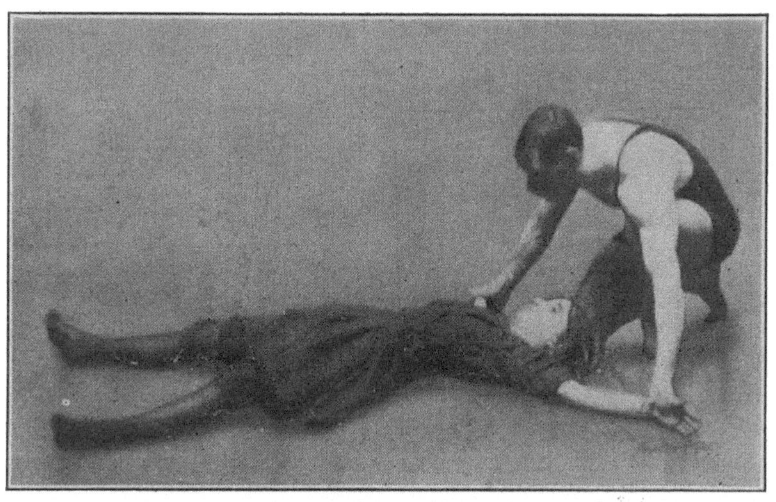

FIGURE 2

as possible, the toes being pointed out straight (Fig. 5). Next the pupil brings the legs sharply together until the heels touch, the toes being turned out (Fig. 6). After these movements have been repeated several times the pupil can try the arm and leg movements together. The arms and legs are drawn up together as in Figs. 1 and 4, then the pupil straightens out the arms and legs, as in Figs. 2 and 5, finishing the stroke by bringing the arms and legs sharply together, as in Figs. 3 and 6.

When these movements have been mastered

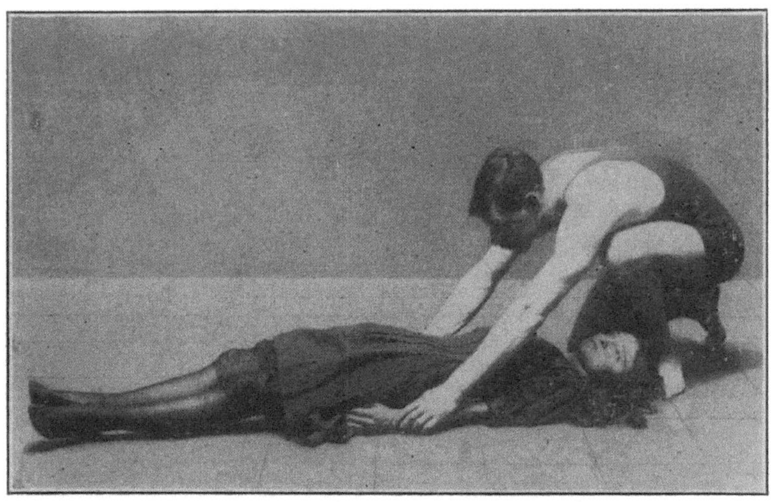

FIGURE 3

by the pupil, I take him or her into the water, waist deep, putting one hand under the back, the other under the chin, forcing the pupil backward until the ears are under the water, then bringing the pupil's hands to the sides, and slowly starting the movements. After the arm movements are mastered, I take up the leg movements, care being taken that the knees do not come out of the water.

To teach pupils how to regain their feet, I show them how to bend forward from the waist until the face is under water, then the pupil will find his or her feet slowly sinking;

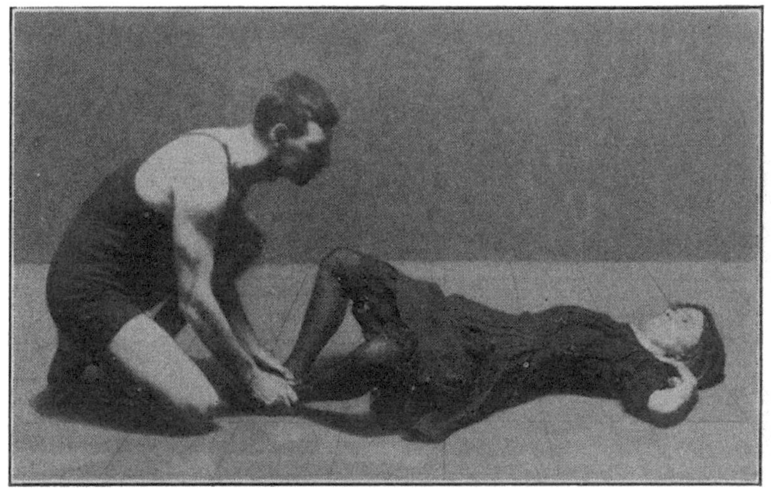

FIGURE 4

when the toes touch the bottom the head can be raised out of the water.

To accustom pupils to the water I teach them to open the eyes and mouth under water. This is much simpler than non-swimmers imagine. Care is taken not to open the eyes too wide. At the first few attempts the pupil will feel amazed, on opening the eyes the first time, at the distance of the vision under water. This is a very good thing to know, and helps beginners to overcome fear of water.

To teach pupils to open the mouth under

FIGURE 5

water I place a rubber ring six inches from the surface and have the pupil bring it to the surface with the teeth. By being careful not to attempt to breathe while under water, the mouth may be opened to any extent without the least danger of swallowing water.

It is wonderful the amount of confidence instilled in a novice on realizing his ability to open the eyes and keep the mouth open under water.

A preserver tied around the waist obviates the necessity of an instructor holding the pupil, and he can, therefore, better direct the move-

FIGURE 6

ments, so that the pupil, while being held up by a preserver, makes headway, care being taken to do the movements slowly and together. Then the pupil is shown how to turn around. The knees should be drawn up, as in Fig. 4, and then to turn to the left, use the right arm only, the left arm should be held in a straight line with the shoulder; then continue to use the three arm movements with the left arm, until one has turned completely around in the water. To turn the other way, use the other arm.

Next the pupil is shown how to float. The knees are drawn up and turned out, the

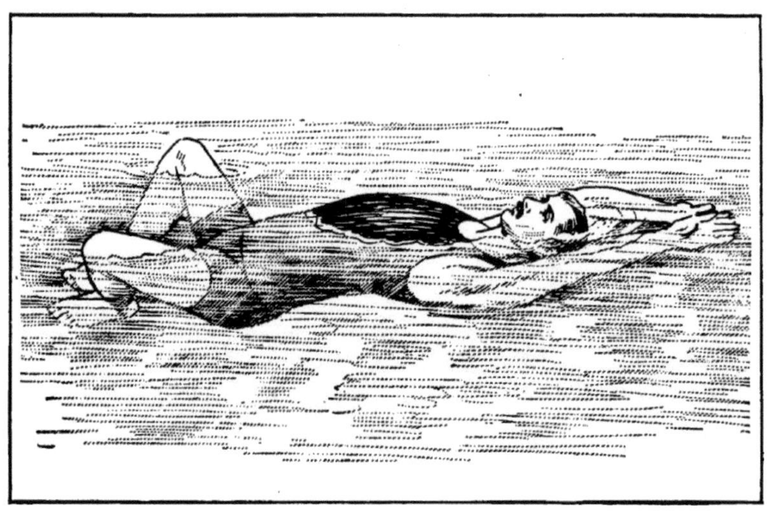

FIGURE 7

arms extended back beyond the head, as in Fig. 7; the hands, about six inches apart, are kept under water. Deep breaths should be drawn through the mouth and forced into the lungs. The pupil will notice that, at each inflation of the lungs, the body will rise in the water, and sink correspondingly when the air is expelled. This practise shows how buoyant the body is. The more limp one lies, the more buoyant the body becomes.

Since I started the Dalton Swimming School twelve years ago, at 23 West 44th Street, New York City, I have always shown my method of teaching swimming scientifically, which is exactly the reverse of the methods of other instructors; that is, teaching pupils how to swim on their backs first, before teaching them the breast stroke, which I contend is the hardest stroke of all, when done correctly. Another innovation of mine is the use of the Dalton nose-clip, a clip that pinches the nostrils tightly together, keeping the water out of the nose and forcing the pupil to breathe through the mouth, which is the correct way of breathing while swimming. The more air one gets into the lungs the lighter one is in the water, making swimming easier. That is the reason so many would-be swimmers, simply because they try to breathe through the nose, get winded very quickly. The main thing about breathing in all the strokes is to keep the mouth open all the time. With the mouth open, air can come in and out of its own accord and the pupil does not have to worry about the breathing.

In my next lessons I teach pupils my own stroke—that is, the Dalton stroke. This is employed when on the back, only instead of going head-first through the water, as in the back stroke, the pupil goes feet first. The legs are

FIGURE 8

held out perfectly straight, then one leg is dropt down in the water, the upper half of leg from knee to thigh remaining stationary (Fig. 8). Then, as that leg is drawn back to its original position, the other leg is brought down in precisely the same manner, the dropping of both legs alternately in much the same way as when walking. To do this effectively, pressure must be applied to the positive stroke; that is to say, while the foot is being drawn down. The reverse movement, or straightening of the leg, must be made gently. The knees should be brought to the surface of the water each time; this is in a slow but restful movement. The arm movements consist of having arms straight alongside the body, the palms of the hands being turned out, the thumbs down, making small circles with the hands and wrists, as in Fig. 8, propelling one's self ahead with small scoops. It is hard at first to combine the two arm and leg movements, but practise makes perfect; and after the movements are accomplished in unison the pupil will find this a very easy and restful stroke.

THE BACK AND DALTON STROKE

In teaching this stroke I revise both the back and the Dalton stroke with the life-preserver on. After the pupil has covered a distance with the back stroke, instead of making a turn to retrace, I show the pupil how to revert to the Dalton stroke, thus avoiding the necessity of turning around. When changing from the back stroke to the Dalton stroke the legs should be brought together and the hands put straight to the sides of the body; then either stroke can be continued. The next move is to let a little air out of the life-preserver. The pupil then begins again on the same strokes. After several trips up and down the pool more air is let out, with more trips up and down the pool, and so on until there is no air left in the preserver.

So slight will be the difference that the pupil will hardly notice it. As long as the back is well hollowed, the upper part of the body will float, but directly the body is doubled up the head and feet begin to sink, so that the teacher must follow close after the pupil to make the pupil keep the back well hollowed and the chest expanded. Beginners will be surprized at the ease with which back strokes propel the body through the water without any undue effort. To one who has never been used to swimming without support it gives a wonderful feeling of exhilaration to propel one's self through the water and then, when tired, to slowly bring the arms back under water until the thumbs come together behind the head and the knees are drawn up to the floating position, while the pupil inhales deep breaths through the mouth, thereby sustaining the body well up in the water.

THE BREAST STROKE

THE breast stroke has been handed down from an early Roman period. It is the oldest of all strokes, but it is the hardest to learn

FIGURE 9

properly, as the head has to be supported clear of the water. Any part of the body when held above water is dead weight, and as the head is all bone, muscle and brains, it is the heaviest part. This is why, in using the breast stroke, it is much harder to keep the mouth and nos-

FIGURE 10

trils above water. The breast stroke is so universally identified with swimming that every beginner wants to learn it. It is only on this account that I teach the breast stroke.

In order to make this stroke clear to beginners I have divided it into four movements each, for the arms and legs. It is a good plan

FIGURE 11

to practise these movements first out of the water. Get the pupil to stand behind, or by the side of, the instructor, and so follow the arm movements. Let him start by having the palms of the hands together, just below the chin, the elbows dropt down and within a few inches of each other, as in Fig. 9. In the first movement shoot the arms straight ahead, holding the hands together, as in Fig. 10. In the next movement turn the hands till the palms are turned slightly out, with the

FIGURE 12

thumbs touching and pointed downward. In the third movement bring the straightened out arms around in line with the shoulders, as in Fig. 11. In the fourth movement bring the hands together till the palms touch, the elbows being dropt, and the wrists touching the chest, as in Fig. 9.

When the pupil has become accustomed to using the arms, the leg movements are taught, each leg separately. The heels are brought together and the toes turned out. Then the left leg is drawn up to the body, the knee turned out, as in Fig. 9. This leg movement is simultaneous with the arm movement, as in Fig. 9. Then the leg is kicked straight out sideways from the body and brought smartly back alongside the other leg, as in Fig. 12. These two movements of the leg are performed while making the one movement of the arm, as in Fig. 10. The arm movements from Fig. 10 to Fig. 11 are accomplished while the legs are stationary, as in Fig. 11. Then the left knee is drawn up, as in Fig. 9, while the hands are brought back to the chest, as in the same figure.

After a little practise with the left leg, the

same movements are practised with the other leg and arms. It is hard to practise the arms and both legs together out of water, as in order to do so one has to lie on a piano stool or bench. I discourage this method because the pressure on the abdomen is injurious. After some practise of these movements out of water, we then take the pupil into the water. When the beginner enters the water, it is best for him to be held in a horizontal position by an overhead trolley attached to a belt strapped around the waist, or else held up in the water by the instructor, as per illustration. The four arm movements are tried first, care being taken that the hands do not come out of the water. At the same time they should be kept as near the surface as possible without splashing, care being taken that, on the last movement, the elbows are dropt and the hands kept up in the water. This movement keeps the head up in the water. Should the hands be dropt, the head will sink. The pupil should keep his mouth open all the time, not worrying whether the water enters or not. By this means breathing becomes natural.

The leg movements are then taken up. The

THE BREAST STROKE—TEACHING WITH TROLLEY AND INSTRUCTOR

best way is for the pupil, with the left hand, to hold onto the rail that lines the pool and to use the palm of the right hand lower down in the water, against the side of the pool, as in Fig. 13, thereby holding the body and legs up

FIGURE 14

in the water, if the back is arched. The legs should be drawn up, the knees and toes well turned out, and the legs then kicked straight out and brought smartly together. This combined movement forces a wedge of water to be shot behind the legs, forcing the body ahead. The legs are kept stationary for a moment and then drawn up to the starting position.

FIGURE 13—THE LEG MOVEMENT

After practising these movements it is a good plan for the pupil to throw himself gently on the water with his face submerged, and so do the leg movements alone, the arms being held straight in front a couple of inches below the surface. As long as the head is under water the legs will not sink. It is

FIGURE 15

surprizing the confidence one gets in doing these leg movements with the face under water. It takes away all fear, especially if the eyes are kept open. When the pupil's breath gives out, he or she should bend backward by hollowing the back, bringing the arms around in line with the shoulders, when the feet will slowly sink and the pupil can easily regain a standing position.

When the arm and leg movements are to be done together, the pupil has to concentrate his mind on the four movements. To start, one must have the legs straight behind,

FIGURE 16

keeping them motionless till the pupil gets to fourth movement of the arm stroke, when the arms and legs should be the same as in Fig. 14. On the first and the second movements, which form a continuous movement for the legs, shoot the arms straight out and hold them there until the straightened out legs come together, as in Fig. 15. Then the legs should be kept rigid, while the hands are turned and the arms brought around in a straight line with the shoulders, as in Fig. 16. Finish the stroke by drawing the legs up and the hands in to the starting position, as in Fig. 14. These combined movements will be difficult at first, as the movements do not go together, as in the back stroke.

When the rhythm begins to assert itself, the best way to practise is with the head under water. Then the pupil can think of his arm and leg movements without the bother and exertion of holding his head above water.

THE CHANGING BREAST, SIDE AND BACK STROKES

To be able to change from one stroke to another when tired without losing one's stride is comparatively simple.

The main points to be observed are to keep the head well down in the water, and continuously use the legs while changing the strokes. Let us assume that the pupil is swimming on his chest. In order to turn to the side stroke he should shoot the right arm in front of the body, giving the shoulders a slight twist, which rolls him over on his side. To turn back to the breast stroke, reverse the movement, using the left arm instead of the right. To turn from breast to back stroke, bring the right arm in front of the body toward the left shoulder, keep the left arm close to the side of the body, and give the shoulders a sharp twist. The body will roll over quite easily. Begin using the arms and legs the moment you get on your back. To turn over to the breast stroke from the back again is harder, and will require considerable practise. Bring the right arm over and as near the body as possible toward the left side. At the same time, give the right shoulder a sharp jerk over toward the left. It is a good thing to accustom one's self to turning over on both sides, both ways. Turning from one stroke to another gets one accustomed to handling one's self in deep water, and is also very useful should the necessity arise for taking one's clothes off in the water.

THE SIDE STROKE

THIS means of progression through the water was once considered the best for racing; but since the introduction of the overarm and trudgeon, and more recently the crawl stroke for short distances, the side stroke, to a great extent, has been discontinued.

The side stroke is good for long-distance swimming, and is a favorite with women, because they can keep their heads above water and their hair dry. The movements of the arms should be practised out of the water, as they are somewhat confusing at first.

Stand with the right arm drawn in, wrist touching the right side of body, and fingers pointing straight ahead. The left arm should be raised in a semi-circular position, with the hand over the right shoulder, the palms facing out. The right arm is shot straight out and then straight down till it touches the legs, when it is drawn up again to the first position. While these movements are being made the left arm is swept down alongside the body, the arm being straightened out all the time until in line with the shoulders again. In other words, the left arm does one short and one long movement while the right arm does three short movements.

While practising these movements in the water, either with a preserver or when held up by an instructor, the head must be kept well down and supported by the water. Breathing should be practised when the left arm is swept alongside the body, as this movement tends to raise the body in the water enough to enable breathing—that is, take a quick, short breath when the arms are being used and so shoot the swimmer ahead.

The pupil should get into the habit of counting the movements of each stroke, and try to be as deliberate as possible while doing the strokes. The slower and easier the movements are made (this applies to all strokes) the less liable a swimmer is to throw water over his face, the better headway he makes and the longer he can keep up the motion. Fast strokes and splashing always denote an indifferent swimmer. Easy and graceful swimming can only be acquired by taking slow strokes and keeping the hands slightly under the surface of the water, thereby obviating all tendency of pushing the arms through the air instead of the water. Next to learn is the side stroke kick, which is an entirely different kick from the breast and back leg strokes, the kicks of the two latter being the same.

FIGURE 17

After having been held up by a friend or an instructor the pupil should turn on the right side and draw the legs up toward the body, as in Fig. 17, the knees touching; then kick the legs out as far apart as possible, at the same time straightening them; then finish the kick without stopping by snapping the legs straight together again with all the force possible till the heels and toes touch, as in Fig. 18. The legs should be kept on the same level in the water all the time. The kick is much the same as is used in the English and American

FIGURE 18

racing strokes. I would, therefore, advise pupils who desire to become proficient in this stroke to pay particular attention to the kick.

The right leg is the one I always bring forward, kicking the left leg back at the same time. I have found I could bring the left leg farther back than the right one; it is a good plan to practise on both sides, as it is very restful to turn from one to the other.

After some practise the pupil will find himself swimming as well on the left side as on the right. Then the arm and leg movements should be done together. Draw the right arm in, the right wrist at the right side of the body, the left arm straight ahead of the body, with the legs drawn up, as in Fig. 17. The right arm should be shot out straight ahead, the left arm is brought with a downward, sweeping motion alongside the body, and the legs kicked out wide at the same time. The stroke is finished by dropping the right arm down until perpendicular with the body, then drawing it up again toward the side of the body. Finish the sweeping motion with the left arm until you bring it out of the water by the knees. Finish the leg kick by snapping the heel of the left foot and the instep of the right together, as in Fig. 18. When these movements have been well practised together the pupil may reverse them and do them on the left side. This can be easily done when the right arm is accustomed to the sweeping motion and the legs are used to the scissors stroke. A great deal of headway can be made when the movements are done correctly.

When the side stroke has been thoroughly mastered, the pupil, in the natural course of events, has a strong inclination to swim faster, so that in time he may excel speedier opponents. The old-time overhand swimmer lay on the water with shoulder blades at right angles to the surface, the upper arm, when

FIGURE 19

pulling through the water being almost entirely immersed, while in the recovery its upper and heavier part was above the surface. Observation of this fact seemed to prove that it was advisable, in order to gain extra speed, to swing the arm forward through the air, there being less resistance, and the difference in general buoyancy of the body being very small.

This stroke was used to a great extent by such noted swimmers as Nuttall, Collier, Standring and Tyers. It should be learned and practised both on the left and right sides,

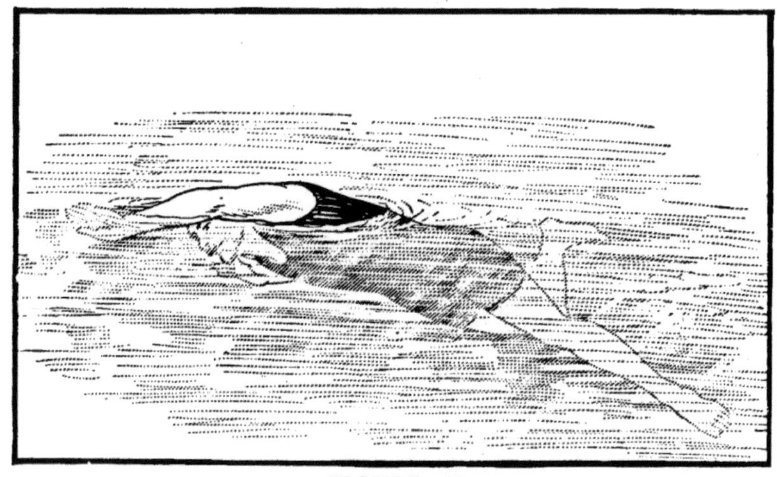

FIGURE 20

so that when the swimmer is tired he can turn from left to right, thereby giving the arms a change of movement and rest. Start on the right side, right arm straight ahead, left arm touching the left leg (Fig. 19), as the right arm is brought down through the water, the left arm is lifted out of the water, and brought over the head and in the water as far ahead of the body as possible, as in Fig. 20. Then, using the left arm as an oar, scoop it down through the water, keeping the arm stiff all the time; at the same time shoot the right arm straight ahead again, as in Fig. 19.

The legs are used in an entirely different way from the breast and back strokes. Keep the knees together, and bend the legs up, then spread the legs and kick them out wide apart, keeping the knees and legs on the same level in the water; finish the kick by snapping the legs together, so that the heel of the forward foot strikes the ankle of the rear foot.

THE ENGLISH RACING STROKE

Before the advent of the crawl stroke the English racing stroke was considered to be one of the speediest of the different strokes. At one time it was used by the most noted of European swimmers. The arms are used as follows: The right arm works as a piston

THE ENGLISH RACING STROKE IN ACTION

rod in and out; that is, supposing the swimmer lies on his right side, as most do, the left arm is cut down into the water both above and away from the head, then drawn in toward the body by a half-circle move-

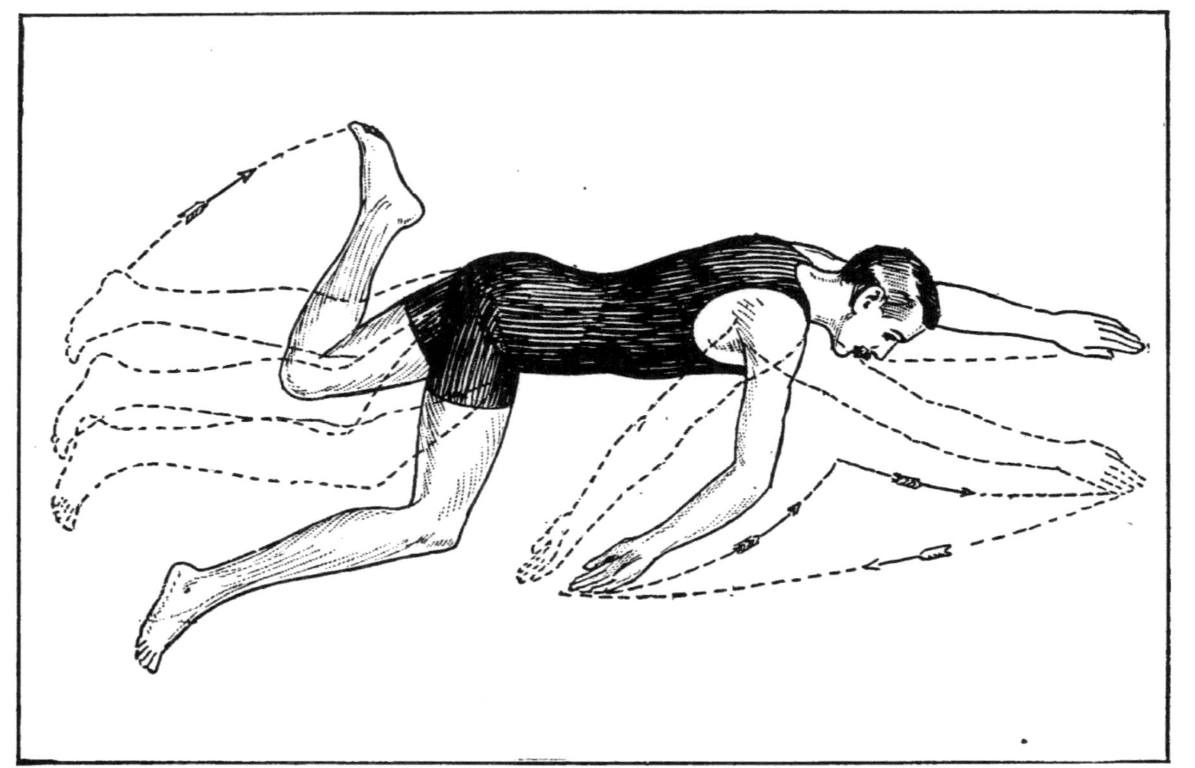

ARM AND LEG MOVEMENTS IN THE ENGLISH RACING STROKE

ment and alongside the body until the left hand comes out of the water again near the knees. The later improvements of this arm stroke consist of using the right arm as a second propeller by bringing the body over on the chest and lifting the right arm out of the water as in the trudgeon stroke. The legs are kicked out together, as in the over-hand stroke, very much as the action of a pair of scissors. The double leg kick con-sists of making an extra small circle kick after the scissor kick is finished. It is very tiring, but effective for a finishing sprint, and is called the double over-arm stroke.

THE TRUDGEON STROKE

The Indian, or "trudgeon," stroke is easy of accomplishment, but very tiring. It is, however, a very effective stroke for short distances. In fact, before the advent of the crawl stroke it was the fastest known to sprinters. Many forms of this stroke are still used by sprinters and water polo players. It was first introduced by J. Trudgeon in England in 1873.

To use this stroke the arms must be stiffened out all the time. Start on the right side, with the right arm straight ahead in the water, left arm touching the side of the left leg; as the right arm is brought down through the water the body must be turned over on the left side, and as the left arm is carried over the water straight ahead, the arms and shoulder should represent a horizontal line, the arms being used alternately in pulling the body through the water.

In this stroke the legs do very little work, the right leg being drawn up and kicked out straight behind with the left arm movement, and the left leg with the right arm movement.

The head should not be held high in the water as the extra weight will make it all the harder for the swimmer to keep afloat. For speed swimming I would advise that the head be kept under water most of the time. The head and chin should only be raised out of the water for breath at each second stroke while on the right side. A good method for using the arms is to bend them from the elbows, cutting into the water over the head and straightening out the arm under water. More speed can be obtained in this way, but the other way is easier for beginners.

THE CRAWL STROKE

Up to the present time the crawl stroke has proved to be the fastest known to sprinters. Indoor pools offer the best opportunities for acquiring it.

This style of swimming was first introduced by Richard Cavill, an Australian champion, by combining with a reduced trudgeon arm stroke the straight leg drive used by the natives of the South Sea Islands. It enabled him to cover one hundred yards in the then sensational time of 58 seconds.

Since that time this stroke has been copied and improved upon by many fast short-distance swimmers. At the present time almost all pupils who take up swimming in earnest insist on being taught the crawl stroke. Unlike other strokes used in swimming, the best-known instructors each have their own variations of this style. The natural tendency of the fast swimmer is to adapt every stroke to his individual characteristics. On this account several well-marked varieties have been developed.

The crawl stroke is somewhat like the double

over-arm or trudgeon stroke, the head and face being submerged most of the time, except when one is taking an occasional breath, when the head is turned sharply to one side. The arms are brought out of the water alternately, then bent at the elbow, and straightened out in front of the head. After this the hand is swept down with considerable force under the surface as far back as the thigh, the body being pulled through the water by the powerful sweep of arms. The legs should be kept perfectly straight, and raised and lowered alternately, very quickly, in a sort of up-and-down movement from the knees. I have found that one can swim a long distance by not using the legs at all. For one hundred yards the crawl stroke is superior to all others.

As this stroke has so many votaries who differ as to its proper manipulation, I hereby reproduce extracts from an able article on this subject, written by L. DeB. Handley, and published in the New York *Tribune,* on Sunday, March 20, 1910:

"Interest in swimming has been growing steadily here, and since the introduction of the crawl stroke into this country there is no doubt that we have advanced more rapidly than any other nation.

* * * * * * *

"In the spring of 1904 the first descriptions of the stroke were brought to the United States by Australian newspapers, and members of the New York Athletic Club thought they recognized in the new leg drive one exhibited by their instructor, Gus Sundstrom, under the name of swordfish stroke. They tried it with their regular arm movements and called the combination the Australian crawl, practising it more as a fad than from any idea of achieving success with it.

"To their own and to every one else's surprize, George Van Cleaf, 'Jack' Lawrence and 'Ted' Kitching immediately increased their sprinting speed with it and were soon traveling fifty yards in record time. The fact became known, and within a short time every team in the country had taken up the study of the stroke. There was established a great school of crawlers, with classes in all the swimming centers.

* * * * * * *

"On his return from the Olympic games of 1906, C. M. Daniels brought the information that the Australian crawl, which he had seen demonstrated by some of Sydney's best exponents, was totally different from our interpretation of it.

"The result may be imagined. Half the crawlers made haste to find out where they were wrong and modified their stroke immediately. Others, however, insisted that our method was an improvement on the other and refused to change. Daniels himself decided

MID STROKE OF THE AUSTRALIAN CRAWL

that a combination of the two would best suit his natural faculties, and so the confusion increased.

"H. J. Handy, of Chicago, added to it by introducing another type, the legless crawl, built on the principle that the kick in swimming does more harm than good. Then came Sullivan's crawl, which is a mixture of crawl and trudgeon, and finally a few extremists took up the amble crawl, which admirers of the late 'Barney' Kieran, of Australia, have been advocating.

* * * * * * *

"As late as 1904 experts were having a hard time persuading those who clung desperately to the side stroke that the trudgeon was the best for all around work, and the fastest

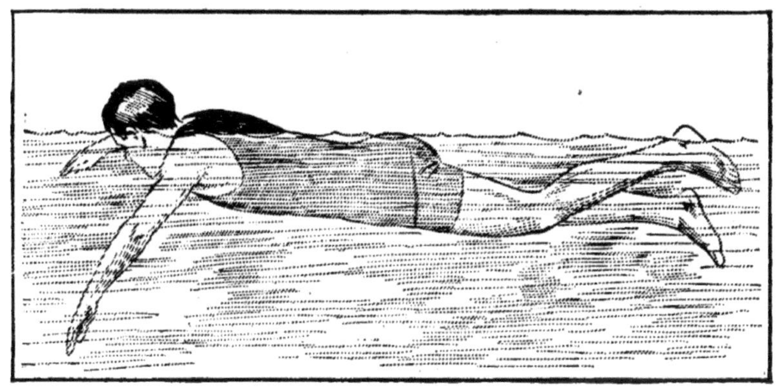

THE SULLIVAN CRAWL

for distance swimming as well as for sprinting. To-day the man using the side stroke in racing is considered a joke, and in the last year almost every national championship has been won by men swimming the crawl. Even the ten-mile Marathon went to a crawler.

* * * * * * *

"The Australian crawl can be distinguished by a short arm reach, with bent elbows, similar to the arm action used in sprinting fast with the trudgeon; by an alternate bending of the legs to a kneeling position and a hard snapping down of them in time with the catch of the opposite hand, and by a flat, face down position of the body.

"Its great advantage is the remarkable speed of action, which allows absolutely no check, making it probably quite as fast a stroke for short dashes as any known. Its worst fault is that it is a freak stroke, totally unfit for distance work. It is impossible to hold it if the movements are fast, and there is no speed in it when they are retarded.

"The American style calls for a longer reach in sprinting; decidedly longer in distance swimming. The legs perform the same alternate thrash, but so much narrower that the feet seldom rise above the surface. The great difference between it and the Australian variety lies in the fact that the movements of arms and legs are totally independent of each other. The body assumes the same position at the start, but rolls a little more, offering a better chance to breathe with less exertion.

"The claim is made for it that the independent action permits one to ask each part of the body to do as much work as it can without strain and without waste. In the Australian crawl the man with weaker arms than legs must either overexert the former or not obtain from the latter their full benefit, for they are timed together. In the American they are taxed with work proportionate to their capabilities, besides which the leg drive is continuous, and can be slowed down as much as one pleases without giving a check, thus qualifying for distance swimming.

"Sullivan's discovery is a slight modification of the American crawl, and in spite of

THE AMERICAN CRAWL

its success it has been called retrovertive. It is the introduction of a very narrow, snappy, scissor kick, as used in the trudgeon, into the leg thrash. It looks in action merely like a wider and more energetic thrash, taken just as the upper arm starts on its downward course, but it gives to the body a sudden leap forward, the speed of which the continued leg drive seems to maintain.

* * * * * * *

"Daniel's combination of the Australian and American crawls was made by himself to find a stroke that would enable him to adapt Cavill's style to his own personal idiosyncrasies. While he considered the synchronous timing of arms and legs and wide thrash the most effective, he realized that a long reach and slow action came best to him, and knowing that slow action in the stroke of his choice meant 'no speed,' he added a slight thrash after each downward slap of the legs, thus making the drive continuous.

"With this composite stroke he did wonders at one hundred yards, eventually creating in England that extraordinary world's record of 55 2-5 seconds. And, of course, as success always draws, he soon had a large following, and many are still using his invention, tho he himself has abandoned it. The fact that Daniels shifted will be taken as evidence that his stroke was defective, but until his great performance has been bettered the thought must recur that for one hundred yards no faster stroke has been found. At the same time, it must be admitted that in narrowing his leg drive Daniels came down to a stroke strongly reminiscent of both the pure American and Sullivan varieties, and that he was able with it to lower by fully three seconds Kiernan's 220-yard mark of 2 minutes 28 3-5 seconds, often declared by experts to be the best world's swimming record in existence.

"Handy's legless crawl is similar to the American in action, but the legs, instead of thrashing up and down, are left limp and trailing.

"It may be remembered that Kieran, than whom no better distance swimmer ever lived,

DANIEL'S CRAWL

attributed his wonderful records, most of which still stand, to his habit of rolling so heavily in the trudgeon that his mouth came above water on either side, thus enabling him to breathe twice where the average swimmer breathes once. He held that proper oxygenation of the lungs was the secret of endurance, and certainly his success seemed to justify his contention.

"The school of amble crawlers uses the

Australian stroke, timing the downward swoop of the right leg with the catch of the right arm and the same on the other side, producing a rolling, floundering advance that looks ridiculous to our unaccustomed eyes and does not seem to have speed. But it is early to judge, for it will take several years to obtain definite results. If there is anything in

THE AMBLE CRAWL STROKE

the theory, it will come to light; our coaches will see to that. Meanwhile, it is worth suggesting that the double breathing would fit into the American crawl much better than it does into the Australian.

"When all is told, it is to the legs that we must look for progress. So far, every leg drive invented has shown the same fault, a decided check on the recovery. And yet we have in our legs far more power, infinitely more strength, than in the arms. Why should the day not come when movements to take advantage of this power will be discovered? The arms are probably working close to their limit, and we have discovered the position for the body that offers least resistance to the water, but the legs are still a negative quantity. When we solve the problem of how to use them, then we will be approaching the perfect stroke, the stroke that will give the limit of speed and endurance to our watermen."

PART III

FLOATING, DIVING AND SCIENTIFIC SWIMMING

FLOATING, DIVING AND SCIENTIFIC SWIMMING

TREADING WATER

TREADING water is a very useful and necessary adjunct to swimming, especially so to the person who either falls overboard or goes to the rescue of a drowning person, or when trying to remove one's clothes. In the game of water polo, also, this method of swimming is practised a great deal.

To tread water is like running up-stairs rapidly; the legs have to be brought up and down all the time; the hands should be kept on the surface of the water, the palms continually pressing against the water, and thereby helping the legs to hold the body up.

It is possible to stand perfectly still in deep water, it being merely a question of balance.

Stand perfectly still, with the arms in line with the shoulders and the head kept well back in the water. The head will sink below the surface once or twice until the proper balance is reached. When this is attained try breathing through the mouth. The swimmer can stand still for an indefinite period.

TREADING WATER

FLOATING

Floating on the surface of the water is enjoyed immensely by all good swimmers. This feat may seem quite simple, but it is not very easily accomplished. There are many persons who are fairly good swimmers, and yet are unable to float properly. The best of swimmers have often attained this feat only after long and persistent practise. It is possible to learn to float without being able to swim, but in that case only by persons not subject to the least nervousness. As a means of securing rest during exercises in the water, floating gives an ideal position. Without the ability to float one lacks the absolute self-confidence in the water so necessary in order to perform numerous aquatic feats.

As a rule, women learn to float more quickly than men, because their bones are lighter. Oftentimes women are able to float the first time they enter the water. Strange as it may seem, while this accomplishment is a very difficult matter for some men to master, with women it is almost natural. Nothing is more enjoyable to a good swimmer than floating. Especially is this true while bathing at the seashore, when the sea is often rough and the breakers high.

The positions for floating or for swimming on the back is practically the same, the only difference being that in floating the body lies

FLOATING POSITION

perfectly motionless, while in swimming on the back the limbs are constantly in motion. There is no position more comfortable to a swimmer than floating; it is the position of rest, and no bed is so soft as the ocean. To be able to lie perfectly at ease with only the toes and the lower part of the feet peeping above the water is one of many pretty accomplishments in swimming. Yet it requires considerable practise to become perfect in the art.

After the novice has mastered the back stroke, it is essential that he should learn how

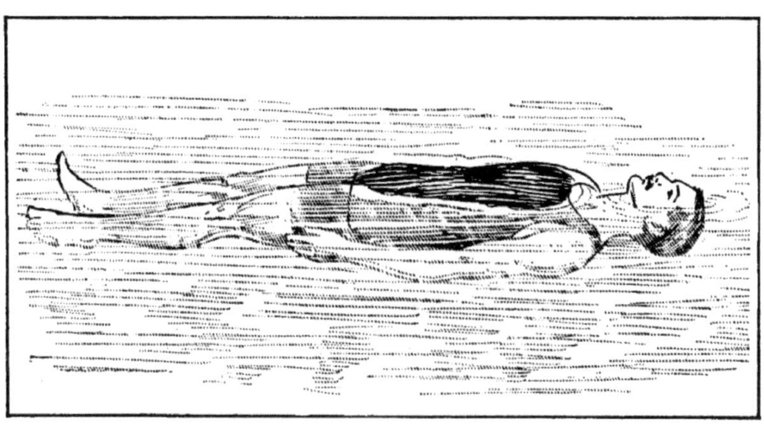

INCORRECT FLOATING POSITION

to float in different positions. Begin then by extending the arms above the head, thumbs locked, and back hollowed; then bend slowly backward until the back of the hands and head rest in the water, when, by giving the feet a slight push forward, the legs will rise slowly to the surface. Keep the mouth open and breathe deeply, as the more air injected into the lungs the higher the body will float. The head, being the heaviest part of the body in the water, should therefore be kept well back. Should the legs show a tendency to sink, extend the straightened out arms under the surface in line with the body above the head; this will counterbalance the legs.

Another method is to draw the heels up

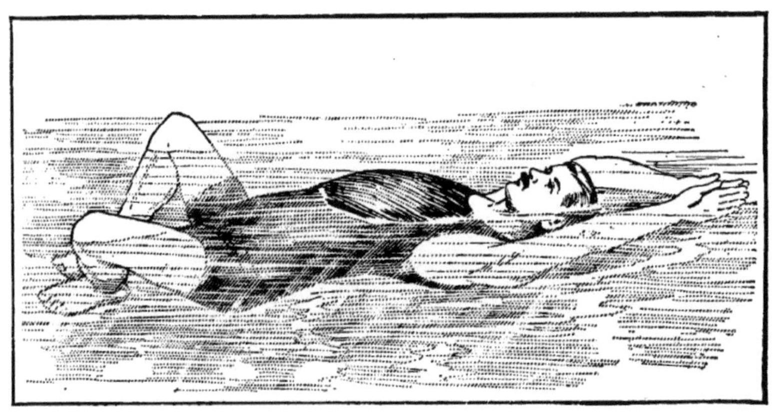

EASY FLOATING POSITION

close to the body, spreading the knees wide apart so that the heels will touch each other. Should the body roll from side to side, spread the arms until the body is steadied; sometimes a slight stroke from the side which is rolling is sufficient to maintain the balance. As women float much easier than men on account of the smallness of their bones, stout persons are more buoyant in floating than slim ones. Floating in fresh water is more difficult than in salt water. Few male swimmers can float in fresh water at all.

To regain the feet in floating seems to be a difficult thing for beginners, and yet it can be done with comparative ease and little splashing if the arms are brought in front, using the hands as a scoop while pulling the body forward from the waist up. By bringing the body and the head forward until immersed, the legs will be forced to the bottom. One thing beginners should always remember is to keep the lungs well inflated and the head well back in the water; in fact, everything should be kept under water with the exception of the mouth and the nose.

Another important thing to remember in floating is to keep the body limp, and breathe naturally and regularly.

DIVING

After a person has mastered the first rudiments of swimming, such as the back, breast, and floating strokes, he is naturally anxious to learn to dive. There is nothing more fascinating to a swimmer than a sharp, clean plunge into cool water.

The whole secret of diving is the possession of plenty of pluck and self-confidence. One need not be an expert swimmer to be a good diver. In fact, some persons can dive very well and at the same time are mediocre swimmers. As in other branches, practise makes perfect.

While in ordinary swimming diving is indulged in merely for the pleasure derived therefrom, in racing diving is a very important factor. Frequently races are won mainly from the ability of the contender to dive properly; in other words, to get away with a skimming plunge, thus securing a good start and getting into a stride that carries him to victory.

This form of swimming is also of the utmost importance in the matter of life-saving.

As a luxury in sea-water bathing nothing equals a plunge from a good height.

I advise beginners to practise from a float or springboard, the latter being preferable, as the spring naturally throws the legs up into the air, thereby preventing the diver from landing flat on his stomach, as most beginners usually do. The essential points to be considered in diving are to keep the head well tucked in between the extended arms, the thumbs locked, the arms forming an arch above the head. In standing, preparatory to the dive, the knees should be slightly bent, so that the spring comes from the bended knees and toes.

In teaching diving to a nervous pupil, at first I generally hold up the left leg as he is bending over to dive. The farther over he bends, the higher I raise the leg, as per illustration. Then it is impossible for the swimmer to fall flat on the water; the upraised leg prevents that. This is the way that I advise all would-be divers to make their first attempt. After a while the diver will throw up both legs in the air behind him. To obviate entering the water with the knees doubled

TEACHING DIVING TO A BEGINNER

up, as so many do (see illustration), the toes must be pointed straight up, back arched. Pointing the toes tends to straighten the legs out (see page 94). Another method I use in teaching a diver to spring well out is to hold a long stick across the water, about four feet away and three feet above the diving-board. This makes the diver spring well out and throw his legs up behind him. It is well to impress the diver always to keep his thumbs interlocked. Otherwise, if he should be diving in a shallow place, the hands would spread and the head would strike bottom; locking the thumbs prevents this.

After deep and shallow dives have been mastered, the pupil can take up various fancy dives, such as the "side dive," "standing-sitting dives," "standing, sitting-standing dive," "back dive," "jack-knife dive," "front-back dive," "back somersault," "front somersault," "sitting jump," and numerous others.

The side dive is made by standing sideways on the diving-board, the forward foot turned so that the toes grip the edge of board. When springing out, the back should be well hol-

A BAD DIVE

CORRECT POSITION IN MIDAIR

CORRECT POSITION ON ENTERING THE WATER

lowed and the face turned up, the head well tucked in between the arms.

The "standing-sitting dive" must be made from a good springboard. The diver stands at the edge of the springboard, the arms straight down, with the hands at right angles with the arms, the palms downward. With a slight spring the pupil drops to a sitting position, the palms flat on the spring-board, and the legs straightened out rigidly in front. Thus the impact, assisted by a push-off with the hands, will jerk the diver head foremost into space. The diver then turns over, straightening the body and entering the water as in an ordinary dive.

In the "standing-sitting-standing" dive from a standing position the diver assumes a sitting position as in a "sitting" dive, drawing the knees under to regain the feet again and pushing off for the dive.

The back dive requires a depth of at least five to six feet. The toes should be well up to the edge of the pool and the back well hollowed. This is the main essential; one also must point the toes out well. This is a

MRS. FRANK EUGEN DALTON
POSITION FOR A DIVE

THE STANDING-SITTING DIVE

THE BACK DIVE

very difficult dive and requires plenty of nerve and practise.

The "jack-knife dive" is made from the back-diving position by springing up in the air, doubling the body up from the waist, and throwing the legs up behind, trying to enter the water as clean as possible facing the springboard.

The "dolphin dive" is the straight front dive, only the body must be turned sharply in the air from front to back. The easiest way is to practise this from a springboard about six feet above water.

The back somersault from the springboard requires the swimmer to double up while in the air; the arms should be lowered from the shoulder and bent up from the elbow, and the knees drawn up, so as to make the body ball-shaped, when the turn-over can be made easier.

The front somersault is exactly the same, only with the face forward instead of backward.

For the Australian splash one stands in the regular diving position, springing well out and doubling the body in the air, with the

THE DOLPHIN DIVE

hands clasping the knees. One must keep the head well forward with the toes pointing down.

The "neck dive" must be done from a spring-

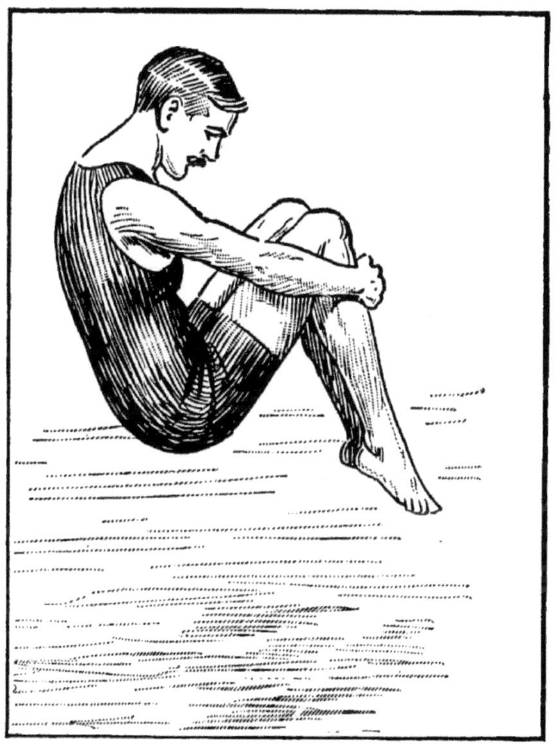

THE AUSTRALIAN SPLASH

board well above the water. Grip the front of the board with the hands, with the head well over the edge, throwing the legs in the air, turning the body over, and back somersaulting into the water, feet first.

When a swimmer has improved and added speed to his racing stroke, he should practise shallow racing dives and how to turn sharply in a tank. This is very important, as many a race has been lost through the inability of the racer to turn sharply when reaching the end of a tank. To practise this, swim slowly to the end of the tank, gage your strokes, so that the right hand grasps the bar which is usually placed around the tank a little above the water. Throw the left arm over the right arm against the marble side of the bath under water; at the same time double the body up. switch around, gathering yourself well together, and shoot forward with the arms extended. Ten to twenty feet can be covered on a good push-off. The method usually followed by swimmers in America is to double up and turn to the left when they are within a foot of the end of the bath without touching with the hands, but pushing off with the feet. In races in England this turn is not allowed, as the racer must touch the end of the bath with his hands.

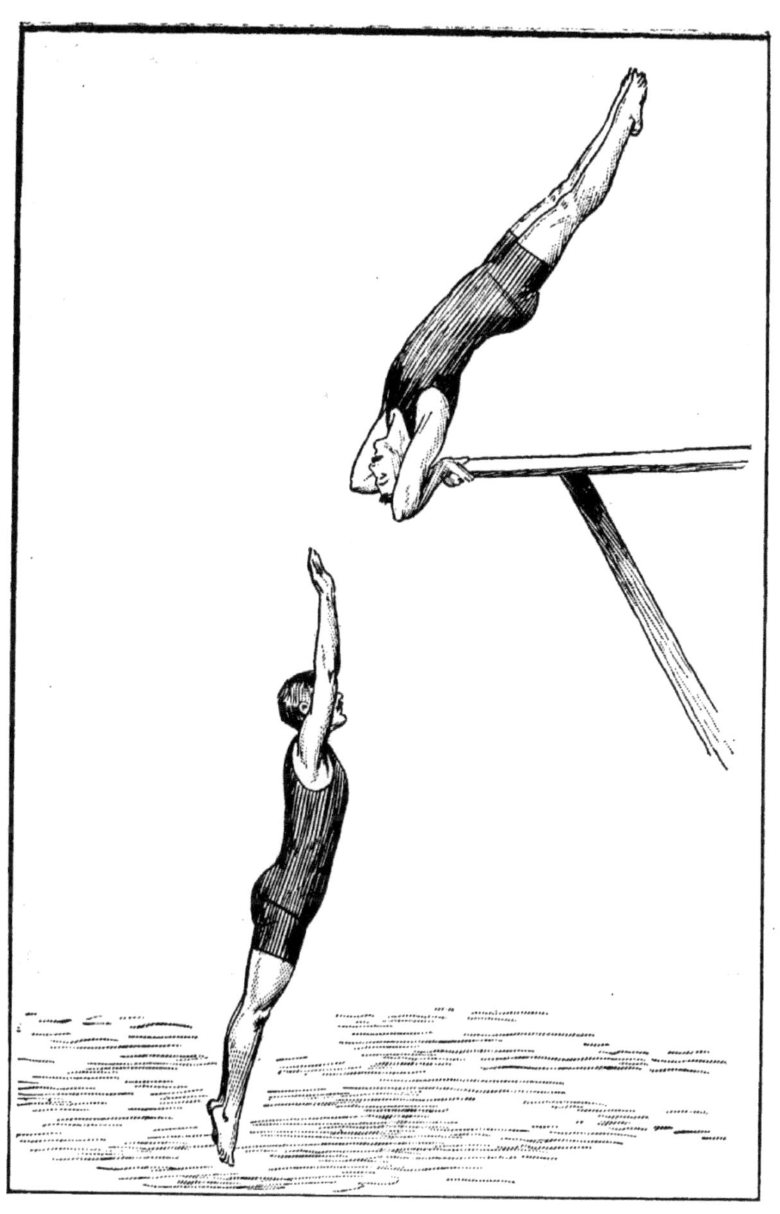

THE NECK DIVE

DIVING

A racing dive is a very shallow dive. The quicker the swimmer gets to the surface. the less time is wasted in getting into his stroke. Both these things are very important and should be well practised. When training in a tank, the racer should never go the full distance, but reserve his speed for the day of the race. In a tank it is a good plan to count the number of strokes required to do the length, so that you know just when the end of the bath is reached without turning the head. A straight course is always advisable. This can be kept by swimming parallel with the side of the bath. It is good practise to get a friend to time your lengths, and get used to diving at the word "go." The best position for a racing dive is with the hands in front of the body, the knees bent, and the mouth open, so that you get all the air possible before striking the water. Always spring out as far as you can. Never mind if it is a flat dive. This is much better than a deep, clean dive, and less time is lost.

SWIMMING LIKE A DOG

Children generally manage to swim like a dog in their initial attempts. This is a very easy and simple method of propulsion, mainly for the reason that the arms and legs are never lifted above water.

SWIMMING LIKE A DOG

Legs are kicked out straight to the rear, sole of each foot striking the water squarely and alternately, instead of working together. Hands are placed in front of the body, with palms down, and are successively brought down under the body and up again.

PLUNGING

To become a good plunger the swimmer, first of all, has to have good lungs. He must be able to hold his breath for at least one minute under water. Ability to float face down, as in the dead man's float, is also essential. Many would-be plungers find that their feet sink after having gone about 25 feet, the reason being lack of practise in floating.

When practising for plunging the take-off should be about three feet above the water. The thumbs should be locked, the knees slightly bent, and the edge of the diving-board gript well with the toes. Empty the lungs by exhaling, then fill again with a long, deep breath, and at the last inhalation spring forward, with all the force possible, taking care not to go deep in the water; about two feet down is sufficient. Keep the head well down and the toes pointing up. The back should be arched and the legs bent up from the knees; this will counteract the tendency of the legs to sink. Unless one makes a straight dive by pushing off equally strong with both legs, the body will go sideways to the side of the pool. Floating on the back and chest is mainly a question of balance, and comes only after considerable practise.

CORRECT POSITION FOR LONG PLUNGE

The time limit allowed in a plunge is 60 seconds without raising the face out of the water. The record is over 81 feet, 5 inches, and was made in England by H. W. Allason.

SCULLING

This is one of the simplest methods of swimming on the back, the forearms and hands alone being in motion during the performance. The swimmer turns on the back with the legs straight out and together, or crossed, the arms being flexible and near the body. The hands, with palms downward, must be in line with the thighs, with the fingers slightly raised. The hands are worked from the wrists, from right to left, in addition to a slight movement (right to left) of the forearm. This forces the body, head first, very gracefully through the water.

SWIMMING BACKWARD ON THE CHEST

In performing this trick of backward on the chest, the body is placed in position as in the breast stroke, the legs and arms together, outstretched in line with the body.

SWIMMING BACKWARD ON CHEST

The feet must be moved slowly from the knees, each leg separately. The feet are alternately pushed backward and the toes extended to the rear. The feet must not come above the water. The action of the hands is performed with the palms facing outward, each hand being pushed alternately forward.

SWIMMING BACKWARD ON THE CHEST

Another method of using the hands is the reverse of the breast-stroke movement; in other words, the breast stroke movement is done backward.

Begin with the arms out straight in front, the palms together, and then draw the arms backward until the wrists touch the chest. Next throw out the arms horizontally in line with the shoulders, the palms turned out, thus sending the body backward by bringing the outstretched arms straight together until the palms touch. If the performer be an expert swimmer he can, by using this arm movement, dispense with the leg movements. This is a "stunt" well worth practising, as it looks very effective in the water.

THE WASHING TUB

This is a very simple performance and requires little practise. The swimmer turns on his back, doubles the body by bringing the knees up to the chin, with the legs crossed. The body is kept in position by working the

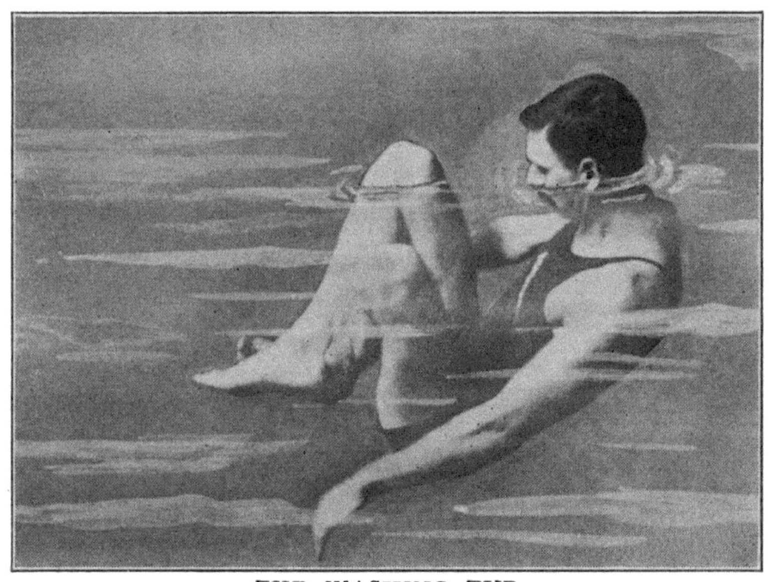

THE WASHING TUB

hands the same as in sculling. As soon as the swimmer has obtained his balance, he pushes the water away from his body with the right hand and uses the left hand in the opposite manner, or, as it were, pulls the water toward the body with the left hand.

THE PROPELLER

This is a very graceful movement and never fails to excite admiration in onlookers. To do it properly requires considerable practise. One must be able to float well. There is always a tendency to raise the head above the proper level, which in turn causes the feet to sink.

THE PROPELLER

To begin, the swimmer should turn on the back, placing the hands at the side of the body, keeping the head back and the feet together. Slight movements of the hands from the wrists will keep the body floating. Then make a long sweep of the arms from the body, under the surface of the water, until they are at full length beyond the head. Thus the body will be propelled with the feet foremost. As soon as the body is in motion, the hands should be moved by the wrists and forearms only, in a scoop-like manner, with the palms turned outward. The body may be turned round by lessening the movement of one hand and increasing that of the other, the body turning to the side on which the lesser movement is taking place. Bringing the arms to the side again as in the original position will bring the body to a standstill. This trick, seemingly very simple, is somewhat difficult of accomplishment, and requires considerable practise.

THE TORPEDO

This is a rather difficult performance. It requires a great deal of practise. The movements are almost identical with those in the "propeller," the main difference being that in this trick the head is kept under water.

THE TORPEDO

To begin, the performer should lie flat in the water on his back, with his arms stretched out beyond his head. The palms should be turned upward. Then the legs should be raised from the hips, and kept rigid. This will cause the body to become submerged, all but the ankles and feet. One then must work the hands the same as in "propeller," but at the end of each stroke make a slight upward pressure with the palms, so that the body may retain its position below the water.

The movement of the hands will cause the body to move forward, feet first. The swimmer should at all times keep his eyes open in order to guide himself in a straight line.

THE CATHERINE WHEEL

This is a very effective "stunt." After assuming the floating position, turn on the right side, with the arms at full length, the hands close to the body, and the knees drawn up.

THE CATHERINE WHEEL

Begin by moving the legs sideways; that is, bring each knee up alternately, straightening out the legs and making a wide sweep with each leg before bringing it up again. The legs are used the same as paddles on a side-wheeler, as in the illustration. This should be practised on both sides. One hand is made to scoop the water toward the body in front, while the other is manipulated the same way at the back. With a little practise one thus may simulate a Catherine wheel—at least when the act is done rapidly and efficiently.

To roll in the water one has to be able to float well; to roll easily the body must float as high in the water as possible. No movements of arms or legs are required at all, the balancing being done with the head.

ROLLING

First get into a floating position, the arms extended beyond the head, the ankles crossed as in the illustration. Then fill the lungs well with air, and gently rock the body from side to side, increasing the motion until the body rolls nearly over on its side. Having reached this position, turn the face well over on the right side, and the body will roll over and turn up again on the other side. After the first complete roll, once momentum is started, the second becomes easier. Several rolls can be made before stopping, provided the breath holds out. Always finish in the floating position. When one has learned how to roll over on the right side, rolling on the left side should be practised, until that movement becomes as easy as the other one. After practise the rolls can be made very easily and gracefully, without splashing. The legs must always be kept crossed and together, never letting the hands come out of the water.

SWIMMING LIKE A PORPOISE

This trick, very interesting and pretty, is quite mirth-provoking to the onlooker, especially if indulged in by a number of swimmers. Unlike the vast majority of tricks performed in the water, it does not call for ability to float well, the only qualification being that one must be a fairly good swimmer.

Begin by lying flat on the water with the face downward. Then take a deep inspiration after having cleared the lungs. As the chest begins to inflate, the body must be allowed to sink under water. At the end of the inspiration the head should go below the surface. After a couple of breast strokes under water, turn the head upward. By executing a strong kick with the legs, the head will rise out of the water. As the body rises, make one stroke with the arms, and, as soon as the head comes up, the arms should be recovered to the first position of the breast stroke and pushed together downward through the water from its level to the side of the body. Simultaneously, as the hands are moving toward the body, the legs should be straightened

SWIMMING LIKE A PORPOISE

with a sharp kick. This will force the head and shoulders out of the water.

A sudden inclination of the head toward the chest will assist the body in rolling over, when the back and legs will become visible after the head is again under water, the legs being the last to sink. By carefully regulating the breathing, this movement can be effected a number of times.

THE PENDULUM

This is another very clever trick, requiring considerable practise; the main essential is ability to float. The "pendulum" is primarily a balancing feat, a well-inflated chest being the main requisite.

The body should first be allowed to float on the water, with the arms stretched out beyond the head and in line with the body. The head must be thrown well back while the body is kept perfectly still. Then take a deep inhalation, bringing the head well forward, as if to look at the feet. Simultaneously with this movement draw hands toward the head. These combined movements will cause the body to sink, and thus assume a perpendicular position in the water.

When the body has assumed a perpendicular position, the arms must be brought to the front of the body, stretched well out, and at the same time the head must be sunk between the arms until the face and arms lie on the surface of the water. When the arms and head are down, the feet will rise and the body float on the surface with the face down.

THE PENDULUM

To come back to the first position, the head must be tilted backward and the hands drawn to the back of the head. Again the feet will sink and the body be swung back to a perpendicular position with the face above water. One must then stretch the arms at full length behind the head, with the palms upward, gradually inclining the head backward until the legs once more rise to the surface, and the body floats face upward.

Repetition of these movements produce a swinging similar to that of a pendulum. The movements must be accomplished with regularity, at all times keeping the legs straight and together.

SOMERSAULTS

This is one of the easiest and simplest tricks. With very little practise it can be mastered by most ordinary swimmers. Of course, this statement refers to the ordinary somersault, either backward or forward, which is nothing

FORWARD SOMERSAULT

more than a turning over of the body while in the water.

In the back somersault the head is tilted back as far as possible, the legs well drawn up, and the arms thrown out horizontally from the shoulders. Then the body is turned on the back and a stroke taken with the arms and hands. As the body is doubled up, this action causes it to turn completely over, the head going under first.

In the forward somersault, the head is prest down upon the chest, the legs doubled up, the same as in the back somersault, the arms at right angles with the body, and the palms downward. The stroke is made similar to that in the back somersault, but the movement is started in front.

If there are a number of these motions to be made, the lungs should be well filled before beginning, as there is no time for proper breathing.

DOUBLE SOMERSAULTS

As this trick requires two swimmers, it makes necessary a great deal more practise. To begin, the swimmers stand on the bottom of the pool, one in front of the other. The forward swimmer throws out his arms at a right angle with the body, even with the shoulders, and spreads his legs until his feet are about twelve inches apart. Then the second swimmer, after taking a deep breath, dives under water and places his head between the legs of the other, bending his legs backward until they come close to the head of the forward swimmer, who in turn tilts his head backward so that it may be grasped by the legs of the other.

When in this position, the swimmers begin to turn backward, using the arms the same as in the backward (single) somersault. The head of each swimmer should be tilted well backward. As the head of the forward swimmer disappears below the surface, the head of the other should appear. After several turns the grip of the legs may be released and the swimmers rise to the surface in their original positions.

DOUBLE SOMERSAULT

WITH ONE LEG OUT OF WATER

In this act the swimmer should lie on his back, the same as in sculling, raise one leg until it is at right angles with the body, keeping the other leg straight and rigid. The action of the hands will propel the body forward.

ONE LEG OUT OF WATER

When becoming proficient in this movement, the swimmer can practise raising the other leg. This requires considerable more force in the working of the hands, so that both legs may be kept in position. By performing the motion of the hands directly under the legs, less difficulty will be experienced.

SWIMMING WITH CLOTHES ON

This is an accomplishment that should be learned by all swimmers. In addition to the sense of security given in time of accident, it is productive of great amusement at race meets and exhibitions, and never fails to excite admiration and wonder in the onlooker. Of course, this can be practised with an old or cast-off suit.

Practise first with a coat, then with a coat and waistcoat; next add trousers, and last the shoes and stockings. This will gradually accustom the beginner to the extra weight of the clothes.

In case of an immersion in clothes, with no help in sight, the sooner the swimmer removes his clothes the longer he can support himself. The easiest way is to float on the back and remove the coat, taking out one arm at a time, using the legs as in the Dalton stroke; next remove the vest, still lying on the back; then unbutton the trousers and pull the right leg down with the left hand. To remove the left leg, use the left hand and kick out with the right leg. To remove the shoes, lie on the back and draw up one leg at a time, crossed over the other leg, and so try and undo the laces. If a knife is handy, cut the laces and kick the shoes off. This is one of the most effective feats practised at exhibitions.

WITH HANDS AND FEET TIED

This trick is most frequently performed with the wrists and ankles tied with a rope. The performer should plunge into the water as for a shallow dive and rise to the surface without making a stroke. The legs are then drawn up until the heels are quite close to the back of the thighs, then the legs are kicked out together. The arms are drawn down through the water, in front of the body, and then shot out. Care must be taken that too much force be not employed, or much of the beauty of this movement will be lost. Naturally, the pace will be slow, but this does not detract from its neatness, nor lessen the admiration that this trick always calls forth.

This work is often performed by experts, having their arms tied to their sides or behind their backs. When performing in this manner, one must swim on the back, and the legs only can be used for propulsion. In this instance better progress is made, as it is much easier to swim on the back with the hand and feet tied than it is to swim on the breast under the same conditions. One of the main essentials in the performance of this trick is ability to float. These performanecs, also, are much easier in a tidal river or stream than in still water, as the body is carried forward with the motion of the water, and less exertion is necessary to remain on the surface.

OVER AND UNDER

This is one of the prettiest exhibition tricks that can be accomplished in the water. If performed by a lady and gentleman it never fails to elicit great applause. The swimmers begin with floating alongside of each other. Then one slowly paddles ahead of the other with his hands until his toes are in line with the shoulders of the other. When in that position, the first grasps the neck of the other with his toes. Then the other slowly brings his or her arms back under water and catches hold of the ankles of the first. After balancing for a moment, the other dips his or her head below the surface, at the same time giving a strong pull at the ankles of the first, which draws the first directly over him. The first one allowing his arms to float straight behind him. While the first is slowly sailing over the other submerged, the latter watches the former, and when the neck of the first is in line with the feet of the other, the latter raises his feet and grasps the neck of the former, who allows his body to rise to the surface. The performance is then repeated

OVER AND UNDER

by the first grasping the ankles of the other, and continuing as before.

These movements must be done slowly and gracefully, each swimmer allowing the other time to inflate the lungs before the next pull-over is made. After these movements have been gone through about a dozen times, and when in position for the final pull, the forward one should loosen the grip on the neck and propel himself ahead to the side of the other swimmer, when both can bend forward in unison, making a very neat and graceful finale.

SWIMMING UNDER WATER

To be able to swim under water is quite an accomplishment and often may be of very valuable service, but as an achievement in competition or for exhibition purpose it is not to be encouraged because of the danger of prolonged immersion, and the fact that many competitors do not know when to desist.

Under-water swimming should be practised by experts only, but care must be taken not to prolong the immersion in order to reach a definite point or to accomplish a certain distance before rising to the surface. It often happens that swimmers, in order to achieve a certain distance, remain under water after pains in the back of the neck give warning of oncoming unconsciousness, in which case they may lapse into a state of insensibility, and there is grave danger of drowning.

When these contests take place in baths, it is not a pleasant sight to watch a swimmer struggling on, against odds, in the hope of beating a rival for the coveted prize. The action of the arms and legs become slower and slower, until at last, from sheer exhaustion, the body rises toward the surface for a short distance and then sinks to the bottom motionless.

One of the advantages of being able to swim under water is the ability it imparts to the swimmer to reach the body of a drowning person, or to bring the body of a drowned person to the surface.

In swimming under water, the ordinary breast stroke is the one used. To swim downward, the head is prest down toward the breast, and when wishing to rise the head is deflected backward.

If swimming under water for a long distance, the body should be kept near the surface, for the reason that the pressure is greater in the corresponding depth. Care should be taken to fill the lungs before starting, and as soon as the first symptoms of asphyxiation are noticeable, the swimmer should rise to the surface.

Among the notable feats accomplished under water may be mentioned that of James Finney, in England, in 1882, who aecomplished a distance of 340 feet. William Reilly, of Salford, an amateur, swam 312 feet under water.

SWIMMING UNDER WATER

The time limit for under-water swimming is about a minute and a half. At the Crystal Palace, London, England, in 1892, in a diver's tank 15 feet deep, Prof. F. E. Dalton picked up 74 plates in a single immersion.

MONTE CRISTO SACK TRICK

This is one of the most sensational performances of the professional swimmer. From a spectacular point of view it is very effective.

MONTE CRISTO SACK TRICK

To do this trick one must be an adept at under-water swimming; an assistant is necessary in order to tie the knots properly.

MONTE CRISTO SACK TRICK

The sack to be used must be large enough to allow plenty of room for the swimmer to move about. At the bottom of the sack place a number of heavy weights. A hole must be cut at the top to allow the rope to be passed through.

The swimmer gets into the sack, taking firm hold of the loosened ends of the doubled rope and that part of the sack close to it. The assistant then takes hold of the ends of the rope and ties them around the sack. The knots must be made on the other side of the sack from that on which the ends have been passed through. After warning the swimmer, so that he may inflate his lungs, he is thrown into the water. The weights at the bottom of the sack will cause him to sink feet first.

After remaining in the sack a few seconds the performer releases the ends of the rope held by him and pushes the sack open with his hands, when he is free to rise to the surface.

This appears to be a very dangerous feat, but in reality is a very simple one for a good swimmer.

NOTABLE FEATS BY CELEBRATED SWIMMERS

Considerable interest was aroused in the early part of August, 1875, when the statement was made that Captain Matthew Webb, an Englishman who had served as second mate on several ships in the Indian and North Atlantic trade, intended to attempt the remarkable feat of swimming across the English Channel. His first attempt resulted in failure. This took place on August 12, 1875. After swimming for 6 hours 48 minutes and 30 seconds, during which period he covered 13½ miles, Webb was compelled to leave the water owing to having drifted 9¾ miles to the eastward of his course by a northeast stream and stress of weather. Webb started from Dover 2 hours 25 minutes before high water on a tide rising 13 feet 7 inches at that port. When he gave up no estimate could be formed as to the probable distance he would have gone west on the tide.

In his second and successful attempt, on August 24 of the same year, Webb started from Dover 3¼ hours before high water on a 15-foot 10-inch tide, which gave him one hour and three-quarters of the southwest stream. His point of landing was 21½ miles from Dover, as the crow flies, but the actual length of the swim was 39½ miles. Very little rest was taken by Webb on the way. When he did stop it was to take refreshment, and then he was treading water. During the whole time he had no recourse to artificial aids. Of this there is indisputable proof. The journalists who acompanied him across in a boat were careful in their observations, and were men whose accuracy could be depended on. The temperature of the water was about 65 degrees. Webb never complained of cold.

For the first 15 hours the weather was fine. The sea was as smooth as glass, the sun obscured during the day by a haze, so that the heat did not affect Webb's head, and in the night a three-quartered moon lighted him on his way. The worst time began at 3 A. M. on August 25th, as drowsiness had to be overcome and rough water was entered. At this hour he was only some 4½ miles off Cape Grisnez, France, and altho he was not then strong enough to strike out a direct course athwart the new northeast stream for land, he was fetching well in for Sangette, where he would undoubtedly have landed between 7 and 8 A. M. had adverse weather not set in. He finally landed on the Calais sands after having been in the water 21 hours 45 minutes. After performing this feat, Webb for some years gave exhibitions of diving and swimming at an aquarium in London and elsewhere. In July, 1883, he came to America for the purpose of swimming the rapids and whirlpool at Niagara, and in this attempt lost his life.

On September 1, 1875, Miss Agnes Beckwith, then only fourteen years of age, swam from London Bridge to Greenwich, a distance of five miles. Beginning her journey at eight minutes to five, Miss Beckwith covered the first mile and a half in 18 minutes. Limehouse Church—a trifle over halfway—was passed in 33 minutes, and Greenwich Pier was reached in 1 hour 7 minutes 45 seconds.

On September 4, 1875, Miss Emily Parker, who had previously undertaken to swim the same distance as Miss Beckwith, not only equalled but excelled the performance of Miss

Beckwith. She went on to Blackwall, a distance of seven miles, the time being 1 hour 37 minutes.

On December, 1899, Captain Davis Dalton swam for 12 hours continuously at the Latchmere Public Baths in London, England.

On August 17, 1890, Captain Dalton left Folkestone for Boulogne with the intention of swimming back across the Channel to Folkestone, a distance of 27 miles. Dalton exprest his conviction that he could perform the journey in 20 hours, and if successful would beat the time of Captain Webb. He entered the water at four o'clock on Sunday afternoon, and accomplished the journey, without any remarkable incident, at half-past three the following afternoon.

In July, 1891, Captain Dalton swam from Blackwall to Gravesend in the River Thames, London, covering the entire distance on his back.

In December, 1891, Captain Dalton swam for 16 hours continuously at the Dover Baths, England.

On August 27, 1902, after several brilliant attempts, Montagu Holbein swam the English Channel, but was compelled to desist when only two miles from the finishing point, after staying in the water for 22½ hours.

The following feats have been recorded as accomplished during the year 1911:

William T. Burgess, of Yorkshire, England, crossed the English Channel from South Foreland, Dover, England, to La Chatelet, two miles east of Cape Gris Nez, France. Burgess started at 11.15 A. M., September 5, and finished at 9.50 A. M., September 6. Time, 22 hours 35 minutes. The distance is 40 miles. Burgess is said to have covered nearly 60 miles, owing to changes in the tide and currents.

On June 11th Martin M. Harris, in an attempt to swim from Chester, Pa., to Market Street, Philadelphia, Pa., a distance of 16½ miles, was forced to retire at Greenwich, after covering 13½ miles in 4 hours 8 minutes.

On June 25th Charles Durburrow swam from the Million Dollar Pier, Atlantic City, N. J., to Ocean City, about 8 miles, in the open sea in 5 hours 33 minutes.

On July 22d Jabez Wolffe, in an attempt to cross the English Channel from Sangatte,

France, had to retire when within a mile of St. Margaret's Bay, England, owing to adverse tides, after 15 hours' swimming.

On July 23d Charles Durburrow, in an attempt to swim from the Battery, New York City, to Sandy Hook, was forced to give up, owing to adverse tides, when 1¼ miles from Sandy Hook, after swimming about 20 miles in 6 hours 43 minutes. About this time Joseph O'Connor swam from Watertown, Mass., in the Charles River, to Cambridge Bridge, Boston, a distance of about 8 miles, in 6 hours 46 minutes.

On August 6th Samuel Richards swam from Charlestown Bridge, Boston, to Boston Light, a distance of about 10 miles, in 6 hours 15 minutes.

On August 13th Noah Marks swam from Chester, Pa., in the Delaware River, to Walnut Street, Philadelphia, Pa., a distance of 16¾ miles, in 5 hours 19 minutes. Miss Rose Pitonoff swam from East Twenty-sixth Street, New York City, to Steeplechase Park Pier, Coney Island, a distance of about 20 miles, in 8 hours 17 minutes.

On August 20th Miss A. Akroyd swam

from Charlestown Bridge, Boston, to Boston Lightship in 7 hours 12 minutes 57 seconds.

On August 27th Miss Elaine Golding swam from the Battery, New York City, to Steeplechase Park Pier, Coney Island, a distance of about 14 miles, in 6 hours 1 minute. Raymond Frederickson finished first in a swim of the U. S. Volunteer Life Saving Corps from the Battery to Coney Island in 6 hours 2 minutes 30 seconds.

On September 3d Miss Adelaide Trapp swam from North Beach to St. George, Staten Island, New York, a distance of about 14 miles, in 5 hours 10 minutes. William D. McAllister won a long-distance swim from L Street bath, Boston, to Spectacle Island and return in 4 hours 50 minutes.

All of these swims were made with aid from tide or current.

PART IV

WATER POLO

WATER POLO

AS A PASTIME

WATER POLO has become one of the most popular and fascinating of all water sports. It can be indulged in by very good swimmers only. It affords abundant opportunity for the exhibition of skill and endurance.

For the following account of water polo the author is indebted to a volume from Spalding's Athletic Library, entitled "Water Polo," written by L. de B. Handley, permission to use it having kindly been granted by the publishers:

The value of an athletic game or contest is determined by four things: Its physical-culture merits; its utility; its attractiveness as a pastime, and its spectacular features.

Water polo has few equals as a means of developing the body. The swimming alone in it would insure general and symmetrical development, but the player wrestles besides, during a game, and every part of the body is given its proportionate share of this gruelling work, developing all muscles in a uniform way.

As to its utility, it is self-evident. Swimming has come to be looked upon as a necessity, simply because it may be the means of saving life, and in this water polo is the most practical of teachers. A player is coached on how to free himself from every kind of a tackle, how to assist an exhausted team-mate and how to apply the best methods of resuscitation when any one is knocked out. Then these teachings have to be practised frequently while the team is at work, and one becomes proficient insensibly and as a matter of course. It is a revelation to see an expert player handle a drowning person, and more especially a frantic one. The rescue is performed in such an easy, matter-of-fact way as to lead one to wonder at the halo of heroism that surrounds most cases of life-saving. Hardly a player but has several rescues to his credit, which he looks upon as a series of trifling services rendered to a fellow mortal, and no more.

As a pastime water polo is among the leaders. Hard and exhausting it may be, but there is an exhilaration in dashing about the pool, fighting one's way to goal, that no other game gives. And it has a feature that appeals strongly to the man who has attained manhood and its numerous responsibilities—the rarity of accidents. Bruises and knockouts one gets a-plenty, but those serious injuries which mar football, hockey and lacrosse are totally unknown.

ITS EVOLUTION IN AMERICA

There is a belief that a game similar to water polo was played by the ancients, but no actual proof of it has been found. Rules were first formulated in England in 1870, and we adopted them in America about 1890, but our present game bears absolutely no resemblance to the one that was then played. In the latter, points were scored by throwing an inflated rubber ball nine inches in diameter through an open goal marked by uprights and a cross-bar; and passing was the feature of the game. Americans found it unsuited. The few available tanks were so small that there was no place for action, and the outdoor season was too short to be satisfactory.

The idea was then conceived of changing the goal into a solid surface, four feet by one in size, and to oblige the scorer to touch the ball to the goal while holding it, instead of passing it.

The innovation met ready favor, but, as may be imagined, transformed the game. From an open passing one water polo became one of close formations and fierce scrimmages. These, at first, were disorderly scuffles, where weight and brute strength reigned supreme, but little by little strict rules were formulated to eliminate rough tactics, and then science became an important factor.

In 1897 a man entered the field who was destined to revolutionize the system of play.

Harold H. Reeder, of the late Knickerbocker Athletic A. C., besides being a good leader and a brilliant individual player, knew how to handle men. He realized that in a growing sport new ideas would mean development, and he made it possible for the members of his squad to experiment with those they had. The system he used is worth a few words of explanation, because it was accountable for the wonderful strides made since 1897, and because every team will profit by its adoption.

Reeder, well aided by Prof. Alex. Meffett, began by teaching every candidate the rudiments of the game; veterans and greenhorns alike were put through the mill. Each was schooled in the principles of swimming, diving, catching, passing, scoring, interfering, tackling and breaking, until these points had been thoroughly mastered, and only then did the team practise begin. But again, no player was allowed in unprepared. Reeder instituted blackboard practise and saw that every one attended it. Placing before his assembled squad the possible formations, he made players selected at random explain the duties of every position in each formation. By this system he obliged every player to use his brains, and he found out the amount of water-polo intelligence that each possest. He also imparted to each the ideas of all the others, he taught them how to fill every position and he brought to light many new plays.

The progress which the innovation was responsible for no one realized until the aggregation of yearlings from the Knickerbocker Athletic Club defeated the formidable array of champions representing the New York Athletic Club. Reeder abandoned the game two years later, but his good work lived after him, and some of his team-mates held the championship for many years by following his teachings

WATER POLO

HOW THE GAME IS NOW PLAYED

Water polo as played to-day in America is rather dangerous for outdoors, and indoor pools are generally used. It is a contest between two teams of six, having as object the touching of the opponent's goalboard with an inflated rubber ball seven inches in diameter, which the referee throws into the water at start of play.

In order to score, the ball has to be touched to the goal while in the hand of a player; it can not be thrown. The goals are spaces four by one foot, situated at each short end of the playing area, eighteen inches above the water level. The size of the playing area is optional, tho the recognized dimensions are 60 x 40 feet or 25 x 75 feet, with a uniform depth of seven feet of water. Imaginary lines are drawn across the tank (see Fig. T), parallel to the short ends, at four and fifteen feet from them. The first, called four-foot line, serves as protection to the goal-tenders and can not be crossed until the ball is within; the other is the foul line, and serves to mark the spot on which the forwards line up on being given a free trial. The four-foot line also marks the goal section, a space 4 x 8 feet, in which indiscriminate tackling is allowed when the ball is within.

Each team of six is divided into a forward line (center, right forward and left forward) whose duty it is to attack the opponent's goal; and a backfield of three (half-back, right goal-tender and left goal-tender), upon whom devolves the defense of the home goal.

At the start of play the two teams line up their respective ends, the referee places the ball in the middle of the playing area and then blows a whistle. At this signal the twelve players dive in, the forwards to make a dash for the ball, the backs to take up their positions. The forward who first reaches the ball tosses it back to the defense men, who hold it until the line of attack is formed and then pass it back. Immediately a fierce scrimmage takes place and either a score is made or the ball changes side and a scrimmage occurs at the other end. After the score the teams line up as at start of play.

Time of play is sixteen minutes, actual,

Courtesy of "Spaulding's Athletic Library."

WATER POLO

divided into two halves of eight minutes each, with an intermission of five minutes between halves. Only two substitutes are allowed, and they can only be used to replace an injured or exhausted player.

WATER POLO

PREPARATORY WORK

No man should attempt to play water polo who is not in the best possible physical condition. Before joining the squad, every candidate, be he a novice coming to learn the game, or a veteran resuming training, should prepare himself for the hard work in sight. I don't mean that he should be down to edge, but in good ruddy health. As a matter of fact, a man is far better off if he can start the season with eight or ten pounds of extra avoirdupois; and four or five pounds above "pink of condition" may be carried throughout the season with good results. They will prevent one's getting cold while in the water and keep one from going stale, a very easy matter in water polo.

Preliminary exercise should be taken daily for a week or two in anticipation of starting practise. Long swims are advisable at this early date, but should be abandoned while preparing for a contest, as one sprints only in a game.

The best system to follow is a very simple one.

A few minutes in the steam-room (not more than five) or some calisthenics to warm up the blood, then a fast hundred. This done, rest until you have regained your breath. Taking the water-polo ball next, pass it to given points of the tank to secure accuracy, and sprint after it each time. Then get against the side of the tank, and placing the ball ten or twelve feet away, try to secure it with one hand on a push-off. This, done half a dozen times daily, will insure accurate passing, catching and obviate fumbling.

Another excellent exercise is to place the ball fifteen or twenty feet from you and then swim after it under water, trying to get it without coming to the surface. This has the double object of getting you used to under-water work and accustoms you to looking for the ball while submerged in a scrimmage.

Gymnasium work is not advisable unless one's physical condition is badly in need of building up, and even then only the lightest kind should be taken. It has too great a tendency to harden the muscles; a swimmer's should be soft and pliable.

Breathing exercises can be highly recommended; there is nothing better for the wind. A good system is to take it while walking in the open air. By inhaling for the space of six steps, and exhaling for six, the lungs are properly worked. In cold weather breathe through the nose.

HOW TO DEVELOP THE NEW PLAYER

The game of water polo is such a strenuous one that even the best of men often tackle it with misgivings. The new player should on no account attempt to take part in a scrub game until he has thoroughly mastered the rudiments. The man who goes in against an experienced tackler, ignorant of the means of protecting himself, receives punishment so severe as to give him a completely erroneous idea of the game.

If the candidate has followed the suggestions given above he will be physically able to stand the gruelling, but more is needed; he should be able to take care of himself. To teach him how, he must be taken in hand alone, and shown the various tackles and breaks.

This is best done on *terra firma;* in the water the man will be thinking of the ducking in sight and his mind will not be in receptive mood. It is also essential to make him understand a hold thoroughly before proceeding with another.

Once a man has the movements learned, he

can be put in the water with a skilled player and allowed to practise on the latter, who should let him secure the holds without opposition at first, but gradually increase the resistance until he becomes proficient. If there is no one to coach and no good player to practise against, the new men should work on each other.

Water-polo holds are a good deal a matter of individuality; each man builds up a set of his own, but one tackle and one break will serve as a foundation for all.

To learn the tackle, give your coworker the ball and let him come toward you. When he's a couple of feet off, take a good, hard stroke, lift yourself as high out of the water as you can throw your arm around his neck, and pulling his head down until it is jammed hard against your chest, wind your legs around his body. Then you have him at your mercy, and you can proceed to take the ball away from him. This tackle should be learned by forwards and backs alike; all need it.

The best break known is the following: We will suppose that you carry the ball in the right hand. On approaching your opponent throw your left shoulder forward, presenting a three-quarter view. To tackle you effectively he must use his right arm, as you could easily repel a left-handed one in your position. As soon as his right arm goes up, place your left hand squarely under his armpit and let yourself sink, twisting around, face toward him, as you pass under, and as soon as you are on your back force his body over you. Then plant both feet on him and shove off. In most cases, if you succeed, you will find yourself between your opponent and his goal, where all you have to do is to touch the board for a score.

To use the legs at every possible chance should be a principle of the player. Once an opponent is caught in a good leg-hold he is rendered helpless. Incidentally, the wise player ceases struggling when he recognizes that he is caught beyond freeing. It is an excellent rule also to avoid being tackled uselessly; if a body encounter is liable to let you out best, or will help your side, go into it heart and soul, just as hard as you know how, but never make a senseless sacrifice.

Passing and catching are all important factors in water polo and should be practised constantly. In passing it is well to bear in mind that the object in view is to give the ball securely to one's team-mate. Pass high and carefully; a low throw may be intercepted and a hard one fumbled. Specially in close quarters high passing is essential.

To cover one's opponent when the other side has the ball and get away from him when one's own has it, should be the religion of every player. In covering him, always stay back of him, where you can watch him, and tackle him just in the nick of time if the ball is passed to him.

Many new men have an idea that one knows intuitively how to score, but it is not so. The various ways must be learned. One only does in a game what one has become used to in practise, for there is little time or chance to think in the excitement of a keen contest, and it is those things which have been ground into one by dint of repetition that stand by one. To get used to scoring, place yourself three or four yards from goal and then sink yourself, or let some one else put you under, and try to come up and hit the board with eyes closed; you will soon find what a difference practise makes. You must also learn how to hurdle by letting some one tread water between you and goal and score by placing your free hand on his shoulder and lifting yourself over.

A short course of the above, and you will be ready to line up.

A FEW POINTS

On entering the tank for an important game, every player should forget his individuality and submit passively to the orders of the captain. There must be only one head for a team to succeed, and an order should be executed without hesitation and without questioning; right or wrong, the best results come through blind obedience. The man giving the orders often sees an opening that the other does not.

Let no personal difference affect your game; play to win, not to pay off an old score. It is the goals made, not the men disabled, that give one victory, and victory is what every player should seek.

To the forward, discrimination is a valuable asset. When caught in a tackle so far away from goal that getting free will not help you pass the ball at once, don't allow your opponent to punish you. But if you are nailed within easy reach of goal, fight as long as there is breath of life in you. Never mind how helpless the task may seem, a team-mate may come to the rescue at any moment, and then you'll score.

The forward should always play the ball in preference to the man and keep free as much as possible. And above all—play fast and hard.

WATER POLO

AMERICAN RULES

1. The ball shall be the regulation white rubber association football not less than 7 nor more than 8 inches in diameter.

2. The goals shall be spaces 4 feet long and 12 inches wide marked "Goal" in large letters. One shall be placed at either end of the tank, 18 inches above the water-line equally distant from either side.

3. To score a goal the goal must be touched by the ball in the hand of an opposing player and the greatest number of goals shall count game.

4. The ball shall be kept on or as near the surface of the water as possible, and shall never intentionally be carried under water. No goal shall be allowed when scored by an under-water pass.

5. The contesting teams shall consist of six a side, with two reserve men who can be substituted at any time when the ball is not in play. A player withdrawn can not return to play. Only six prizes shall be given to the winning team.

6. Time of play shall be 16 minutes actual time, divided in two halves of 8 minutes each and 5 minutes rest between halves. Time occupied by disputes, free trials for goal, repairing suits, and lining up after a goal has been scored shall not be reckoned as time of play.

7. The captains shall be playing members of teams they represent and shall toss for choice of ends of tank. The ends shall be changed at half time.

8. The referee shall throw the ball in the center of the tank and the start for the ball be made only at the sound of the whistle.

9. A ball going out of the tank shall be returned to the place from which it was thrown and given to the opposing team.

10. A mark shall be made four feet from each goal on the side of the tank and an imaginary line between these marks shall be called the four-foot line. No man will be allowed within this line until the ball is within it. The goal-tenders, limited to two, of the defending side are alone exempt from this rule. When the ball is within the goal-line the goal-tenders shall not be allowed any arti-

ficial support other than the bottom of the tank.

11. No player is allowed to interfere with an opponent unless such an opponent is within four feet of the ball, except when the ball is within the goal section, when indiscriminate tackling will be allowed in the goal section, the goal section to be a space of four feet by eight feet within the goal-line and between two parallel lines drawn at right angles to the goal-line and distant two feet from either end of the goal.

12. Upon a goal being gained, the opposite teams shall go to their own end of the tank, and the ball shall be thrown by the referee into the center and play started as at beginning of game.

13. Each team shall have two judges, one at each goal-line, who, upon a goal being made, shall notify the referee and announce the same.

Only in case the judges disagree shall the referee have power to decide whether a goal be fairly made or not.

14. The referee shall decide all fouls, and if in his opinion a player commits a foul he shall caution the team for the first offense and

give the opponents a free trial for goal at each succeeding foul.

A free trial for goal will be given by lining up three backs of the defending team within the 4-foot line and giving three forwards of the opposing team the ball on the 15-foot line, when they may try for a goal until a goal is scored or the ball goes outside the 15-foot line. Only three men from each side will be allowed within the 15-foot line, until the ball goes outside that line or a goal is scored.

Fouls.—It shall be foul to tackle an opponent if the ball is not within four feet of him or to hold him by any part of his costume. It shall be a foul to cross the 4-foot line ahead of the ball, unless forced over by an opponent, or to hang on to the sides of the tank except for the purpose of resting.

Unnecessary rough work may, within the discrimination of the referee, either be counted a foul or the referee may put the offender out of the tank until a goal is scored or the half ends.

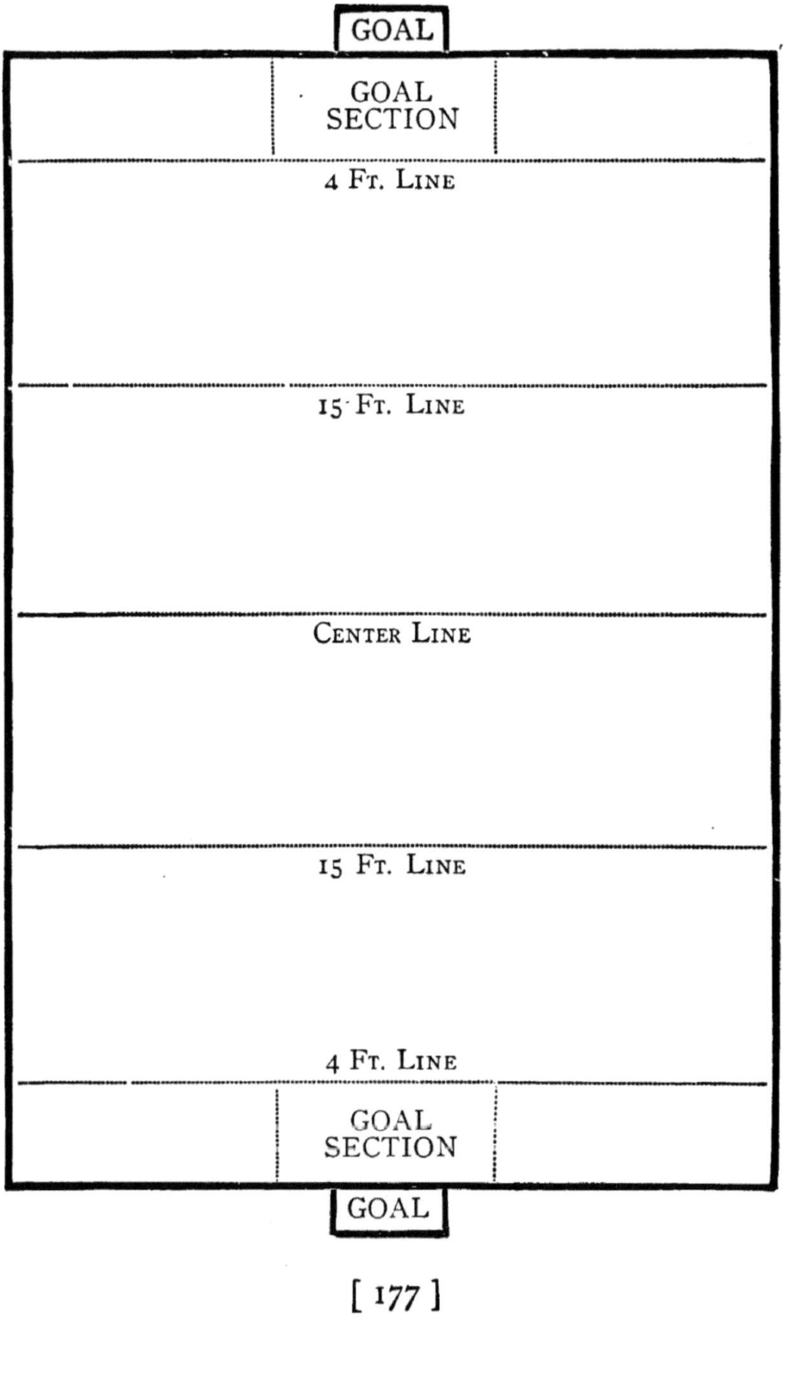

GOAL

GOAL SECTION

4 Ft. Line

15 Ft. Line

Center Line

15 Ft. Line

4 Ft. Line

GOAL SECTION

GOAL

PART V

CRAMPS, HOW TO SAVE LIFE, RESUSCITATION, ETC.

CRAMPS, HOW TO SAVE LIFE, RESUSCITATION, ETC.

CRAMPS

To BE suddenly seized with cramps is a thing liable to happen to most expert swimmers; it is caused by various reasons—staying too long in the water and getting chilled, going in after a heavy meal, stiffening the legs too much, and varicose veins. Preventive: Never remain in the water after feeling chilled; always swim around and excercise yourself; twenty minutes is long enough for any one to remain in the water; always turn over on the back when getting a cramp, and float, at the same time working toward the shore with the hands, and don't lose your presence of mind.

Don't attempt to rescue a person from drowning unless you are a good swimmer yourself; remember that a drowning person is generally insane for the time, and is liable to drag you to your death unless you are capable of swimming with a heavy load.

HOW TO SAVE LIFE

To the person who accidentally falls overboard, or who is compelled to leap into deep water, as was the case with many victims of the *General Slocum,* the first essential is to keep one's presence of mind. Do not feel alarmed if your head should sink below the surface once or twice—you are bound to come to the surface, and will be able to sustain yourself for a considerable time, even if you are not a swimmer, if you will but keep your hands under water. The reason so many people drown is because directly they come to the surface they raise their hands above their head and shout for help. This is fatal. The moment the hands are raised out of the water the body will sink below the surface.

Another thing to remember is to keep the mouth closed until the body attains the floating position; then try and breathe naturally through the mouth and help propel yourself with your hands. Should you be able to swim, try and take off your outer clothing, as the latter, when water-soaked, tends to drag the body down, besides retarding the movements of the drowning person.

HOW TO SAVE LIFE

To risk one's life in order to save a fellow being from drowning is one of the most heroic acts that one may be called upon to perform, yet how many of us have the presence of mind and courage to act in such an emergency? To rescue a person from drowning is no child's play, even for the best swimmers; it requires pluck, nerve and stamina. Of course, I allude to rescues which take place some distance from shore. Many a daring swimmer has been clutched and dragged down to death simply because he did not know the safest way to approach a drowning person.

Of the many different ways of saving life, the safest and best method is to swim as near the person as possible, then dive under and come up behind him; otherwise he is liable to grab you around the neck with a death clutch, from which it is extremely difficult to escape. When swimming up behind the person, grab his biceps and force him on his back; the more he struggles the more he helps himself to keep afloat.

To prevent being clutched by a drowning person the following rules should be carefully studied. Every action, however, must be prompt and decisive, otherwise this method will be of no avail.

1. If grasped by the wrists, turn both arms simultaneously against the drowning person,

THE BEST METHOD OF SAVING LIFE

thumbs outward, and attempt to bring your right arms at right angles to your own body. This will dislocate the thumbs of the drowning person and he must let go his hold.

2. If clutched around the neck, immediately take a deep breath, lean well over your opponent, place the left hand in the small part of

his back and draw your right arm in an upward direction until in line with his shoulder, and pass it at once over his arm. Then with the thumb and forefinger catch his nose and pinch the nostrils close, at the same time place the palm of your hand on his chin and push firmly outward. This will cause him to open his mouth for breathing purposes, and he, being under you, will swallow water. Choking ensues, and not only is the rescuer let go, but the other is left so helpless as to be completely under control.

3. If clutched around the body and arms, take a deep breath, lean well over your opponent and throw the right arm in an upward direction at right angles to the body, or draw it up between your body and that of your opponent. Then with the thumb and forefinger catch the nose and pinch the nostrils close, and at the same time place the palm of the hand on the chin and bring the right knee as high as possible up between the two bodies, placing it, if possible, against the lower part of your opponent's chest; then, by means of a strong and somewhat sudden push, stretch your arms and legs out straight, at the same

time throwing the whole weight of the body backward. The sudden motion will press the air out of the other's lungs, as well as push him off, no matter how tightly he may be holding.

Should the drowning person act sensibly and not try to grab his rescuer, he can be brought in by placing his hands on his rescuer's shoulders and kicking out his legs behind him while the rescuer swims in toward shore. Another method is to pull the person on his back by holding him under the right arm-pit with your right hand and using the left hand and legs to swim with. Should the rescue be close to shore, swim behind the person and help by pushing him in toward shallow water. Should the drowning person have sunk for the third time watch when the air-bubbles rise to the surface. At once dive down perpendicular to the bottom when the air-bubbles show, seize the drowning person and bring him to the surface by pushing off from the bottom and using your legs to send you upward to the surface. Before trying to rescue any one get rid of as much clothing as possible, if time will permit.

RESUSCITATION AFTER RESCUE

After bringing a drowning person ashore your work is only half done; the main thing is to bring him back to life should he be unconscious. There are several methods for resuscitating the apparently drowned. The method adopted by the Royal Humane Society of England is, to my knowledge, the simplest of all. It is as follows:

Begin treatment in the open air as soon as you have brought the unfortunate ashore. Meanwhile send for medical assistance, blankets and dry clothing. Expose the patient's throat and chest to the wind, except in very severe weather. Remove all tight clothing from neck and chest. Take off suspenders.

The points to be aimed at are: First and immediately the restoration of breathing, and, secondly, after breathing is restored, the promotion of warmth and circulation. The efforts to restore breathing must be commenced immediately and energetically, and persevered in for one or two hours, or until a medical man has pronounced that life is extinct.

Efforts to promote warmth and circulation

beyond removing the wet clothes and drying the skin must not be made until the first appearance of natural breathing, for if circulation of the blood be induced before breathing has recommenced the restoration of life will be endangered.

To clear the throat, place the patient on the floor or the ground with the face downward and one of the arms under the forehead, in which position all fluids will more readily escape by the mouth, and the tongue itself will fall forward, leaving the entrance into the windpipe free. Assist this operation by wiping and cleansing the mouth.

If satisfactory breathing begins, use the treatment described below to promote warmth. If there be only slight breathing, or no breathing, or if the breathing fail, then, to excite breathing, turn the patient well and instantly on the side, supporting the head, and excite the nostrils with snuff, hartshorn, and smelling-salts, or tickle the throat with a feather, etc., if they are at hand. Rub the chest and face warm, and dash cold water, or cold and hot water alternately, on them.

If there be no success, lose not a moment, but instantly, to imitate breathing, replace the patient on the face, raising and supporting the chest well on a folded coat or other article of dress. Turn the patient very gently on the side and a little beyond, and then briskly on the face, back again; repeating these measures cautiously, efficiently and perseveringly about fifteen times in the minute, or once every four or five seconds, occasionally varying the side. (By placing the patient on the chest, the weight of the body forces the air out; when turned on the side this pressure is removed, and air enters the chest.)

On each occasion that the body is replaced on the face make uniform but efficient pressure, with brisk movement, on the back between and below the shoulder-blades or bones on each side, removing the pressure immediately before turning the body on the side. During the whole of the operations let one person attend solely to the movements of the head, and of the arm placed under it.

The result is respiration, or natural breathing, and, if not too late, life.

While the above operations are being proceeded with, dry the hands and feet, and as soon as dry clothing or blankets can be procured, strip the body and cover, or gradually reclothe it, but take care not to interfere with the efforts to restore breathing.

SYLVESTER'S METHOD

Rule 1. *To Adjust the Patient's Position.*—Place the patient on his back on a flat surface, inclined a little from the feet upward; raise and support the head and shoulders on a small, firm cushion or folded article of dress, placed

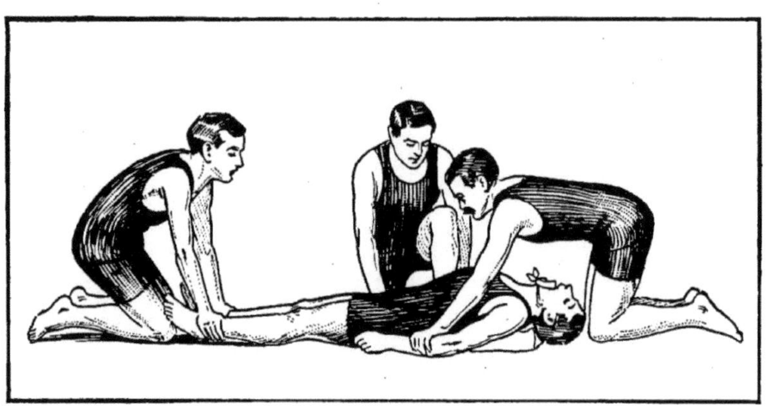

SYLVESTER'S METHOD—FIGURE 1

under the shoulder-blades. Remove all tight clothing from about the neck and chest.

Rule 2. *To Maintain a Free Entrance of Air Into the Windpipe.*—Cleanse the mouth and nostrils; open the mouth; draw forward the patient's tongue, and keep it forward; an elastic band over the tongue and under the chin will answer this purpose. (Fig. 1.)

Rule 3. *To Imitate the Movements of Breathing.*—First, *Induce inspiration.* Place yourself at the head of the patient, grasp his arms (at the elbow-joints), raise them upward by the sides of his head, stretch them steadily but gently upward, for two seconds. By this means fresh air is drawn into the lungs by raising the ribs. (Fig. 2.)

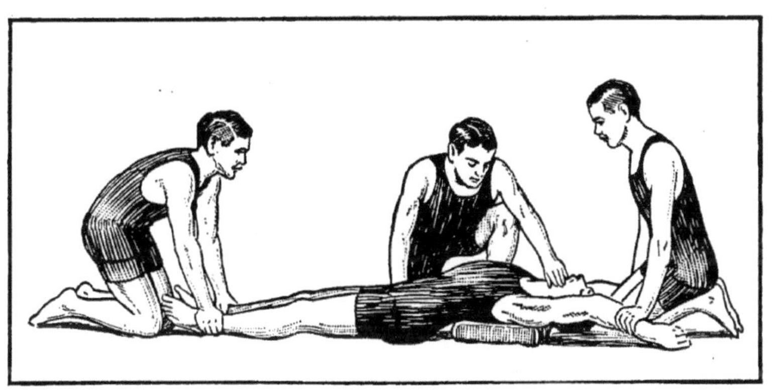

SYLVESTER'S METHOD—FIGURE 2

Secondly, *Induce Expiration.*—Immediately turn down the patient's arms, and press the elbows firmly but gently downward against the sides of the chest, for two seconds. By this means foul air is expelled from the lungs by depressing the ribs. (Fig. 3.)

Thirdly. *Continue These Movements.*—Repeat these measures alternately, deliberately, and perseveringly fifteen times a minute, until a spontaneous effort to respire be perceived. By these means an exchange of air is produced in the lungs similar to that effected by natural respiration.

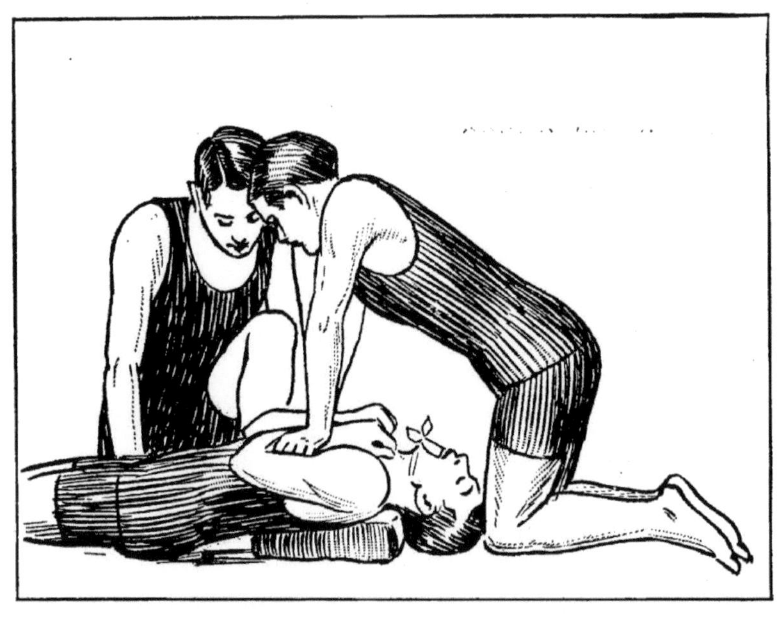

SYLVESTER'S METHOD—FIGURE 3

When a spontaneous effort to respire is perceived, cease to imitate the movements of breathing, and proceed to induce circulation and warmth, as described on following page.

Rule 4. *To Excite Respiration.*—During the employment of the above method, excite the nostrils with snuff or smelling-salts, or tickle the throat with a feather. Rub the chest and face briskly, and dash cold and hot water alternately on them. Friction of the limbs and body with dry flannel or cloths should be had recourse to. When there is proof of returning respiration, the individual may be placed in a warm bath, the movements of the arms above described being continued until respiration is fully restored. Raise the body in twenty seconds to a sitting position, dash cold water against the chest and face, and pass ammonia under the nose. Should a galvanic apparatus be at hand, apply the sponges to the region of the diaphragm and the heart.

To Induce Circulation and Warmth.—Wrap the patient in dry blankets, and rub the limbs upward energetically. Promote the warmth of the body with hot flannels, bottles or bladders of hot water; heated bricks to the pit of the stomach, the arm-pits, and to the soles of the feet.

On the restoration of life, when the power of swallowing has returned, a teaspoonful of warm water, small quantities of wine, warm brandy and water, or coffee should be given. The patient should be kept in bed, and a disposition to sleep encouraged. During re-action, large mustard-plasters to the chest and below the shoulders will greatly relieve the distrest breathing.

NOTE.—In all cases of prolonged immersion in cold water, when the breathing continues, a warm bath should be employed to restore the temperature.

Printed by Libri Plureos GmbH in Hamburg,
Germany